Testin

Saving Ourselves from Suicide

"In graphic, painful detail, the author chronicles the unraveling of her son Nick's short life and the reasoning and rationalizing of choices he and their family made. There are many moments of recognizable parental concerns that can touch those who may wonder about the safety of their own child. A call for compassion that is visceral as the author explains how slights, bullying, ignoring, and ridicule can have a cumulative effect on someone who is suffering from mental illness.

"The author has a crystal clear vision of mental health and the continuums of illness. She connects the lack of understanding that accompanies mental illness with how stigma arises and festers in a real way so that an imperative for education is obvious.

"One thing that stands out in this account is how difficult it is to understand mental illness if you do not have experience with it. Highly educated persons can hold misconceptions and still miss the nuances of family and individual pain and fail to connect the dots.

"*Saving Ourselves from Suicide* is both a personal journey and warning to families. The author is clearly on a mission to save others from the tragedy that befell her family. It is invaluable."

—Christine Z. Somervill, PhD
Director of Programs, NAMI (National Alliance on Mental Illness),
Cook County North Suburban, Chicagoland

"*Saving Ourselves from Suicide* is a touching account of one family's survival after losing their son and brother to suicide. While this is a loss that none of us would wish on anyone, *Saving Ourselves from Suicide* gives a meaningful glimpse into the powerful loss and the many things we can do to support each other and our loved ones through struggle."

—Alison Malmon
Founder/Executive Director, Active Minds

"In *Saving Ourselves from Suicide*, Linda Pacha tells the story of her son, Nick, honestly recounting significant experiences and events in his life and outlining his unique challenges and strengths in an effort to better understand why he died by suicide. Linda gives details about the ways she and her family grieved differently and outlines the methods that they used to cope with Nick's traumatic death, including increasing their understanding of mental health challenges, the role of their faith and spiritual beliefs, and the power of connecting with others who have had similar experiences. The common thread throughout the book is Linda's call for all to be kinder and more compassionate to one another, to search for understanding, and to be aware of how our actions impact others."

—Rev. Charles T. Rubey
Founder/Director, Loving Outreach to Survivors of Suicide (LOSS),
a nondenominational program and division of Catholic Charities

"This book is important on so many levels. It describes the emotional journey of living through the events leading up to suicide and walks through the painful steps of the initial shock and long grieving process. It is a valuable resource to make it through grief and loss. This is a visceral but important read."

—Steve Arkin, MD
Attending Neurologist, Miami Valley Hospital
Assistant Professor, Wright State University, Dayton, Ohio
Cofounder, SpeakUp

"Various kinds and levels of adversity are an inevitable part of this life, but such adversity does not have to result in despair. However, without emotional connection with others and a spiritual grounding, we are left to feel isolated, alone, and ultimately without hope. We as a society have become so relationally disconnected from one another that it has led to despair, resulting in rising rates of depression and suicide. Open and honest conversation about mental health and suicide is needed now more than ever in our society. Through the eyes of a loving mother, this book does just that in a candid, caring, and hope-filled way, providing a needed narrative of one family's journey with the challenge of mental health issues. *Saving Ourselves from Suicide* is a significant contribution to the critical dialogue that we all need to be engaged in regarding how to reduce the stigma of mental health in our society. It is a call to action to turn the tide of despair that is now so prevalent in our culture today."

—Rev. Dr. Scott Mitchell, MTh, PsyD
Licensed Clinical Psychologist
President and CEO, SamaraCare

"Awareness, education, and connection are keys to tackling the overwhelming issue of suicide in our society. The author's voice in *Saving Ourselves from Suicide* brings awareness to a new level through her brave and honest account of the death of her beautiful son by suicide and the impact this had on her family and the community."

—Fran Zucco, BSN, RN-BC
Clinical Leader
Linden Oaks Behavioral Health

"Linda Pacha's *Saving Ourselves from Suicide* draws you into all the emotions and fears that parents experience as they attempt to help their beloved child negotiate the changes, chances, and most certainly the unkind aspects of life. A high-functioning mental/personality challenge, sexual orientation questions, depression, resulting isolation, and bullying and ridicule by peers, classmates, and total strangers set a course that no parent would seek for their child's kind, tender, and formative soul. Linda's story of Nick and his journey draws you empathically into his and her experience. You find yourself at the emotional bottom when Nick makes the ultimate decision that is irreversible. Instead of being stuck there as an end point, Linda continues to write how she finds that the bottom is firm with the ability to rebound in measured steps. Her faith, a hope to heal, love from family and close friends, and their support actually fueled a wounded healer's heart. As part of her pathway to healing, she has chosen to passionately share insights, information, and resources to help others decide to *stay* or to assist the healing of those who have experienced the tragic loss of a loved one to suicide. You cannot heal alone, and her sharing may be the best informed, friendly advice you could receive. It comes from a deep, painful experience and with the authenticity of a mother's broken heart."

—The Rev. Dr. Steven R. Rottgers
Canon to the Ordinary, Episcopal Diocese of West Missouri
Author of *I Am Yours*

"*Saving Ourselves from Suicide* is a courageously written memoir from a mother navigating the loss of her son. Not only is this book a must-read for anyone suffering a loss to suicide, it is also a guide offering support for those living with a loved one who suffers from mental illness. Having survived the loss of my own twin brother to suicide, I can say that the honesty with which Linda shares her journey, describing the events before and after the loss of her son, is both compelling and relatable. Rather than hiding behind the stigma of suicide and weighing the reader down with unnecessary stats and references, Linda's heartfelt storytelling opens the door for us survivors to move through our pain and start healing. *Saving Ourselves from Suicide* reminds us survivors that we are not alone in our grief and together, we can move forward and start living again."

—Monica Pedersen
Former HGTV Host, Author, Interior Designer

SAVING OURSELVES FROM SUICIDE

BEFORE and AFTER

HOW TO ASK FOR HELP, RECOGNIZE WARNING SIGNS, AND NAVIGATE GRIEF

LINDA PACHA

Owned and operated by Nick's Network of Hope, a 501(c)(3) nonprofit
Naperville, IL

All scripture quotations in this publication are from the Good News Translation in Today's English Version-Second Edition Copyright © 1992 by American Bible Society. Used by Permission.

The names and identifying details of certain individuals have been changed to protect their privacy.

Cover Design: Susan Olinsky
Copyedit: Christina Roth
Page Design: Lissa Auciello-Brogan

AutumnBloom Press is wholly owned by Nick's Network of Hope, a 501(c)(3) nonprofit.

Manufactured in the United States of America

Names: Pacha, Linda, author
Title: Saving Ourselves From Suicide—Before and After: How to Ask for Help, Recognize Warning Signs, and Navigate Grief | Linda Pacha
Description: First Edition. | Naperville : AutumnBloom Press, [2019]
Identifiers: Library of Congress Control Number : 2019957802

978-1-7344096-8-0 (hardcover)
978-1-7344096-9-7 (ebook)
978-1-7344096-1-1 (trade paperback)

Saving Ourselves from Suicide—Before and After is also available for purchase for promotional, educational, or business use on the Nick's Network of Hope website, nicksnetwork ofhope.org. The author, Linda Pacha, is the founder/president of Nick's Network of Hope, a 501(c)(3) nonprofit charity that provides resources, education, and support about life challenges with an emphasis on mental health awareness, suicide prevention, and grief and loss.

To my son, Nicolas ("Nick"), a bright light who was the kindest and purest soul I have ever known. He taught me how to look for the good in people. It was always important to Nick to bring more kindness and compassion in this world, and he did so by reaching out and helping others. This book honors his life by continuing his mission, offering information, hope, and solace to everyone who reads it. Thanks, Nick, for showing me that love is truly eternal and transcends any veil of separation.

Contents

CONTENTS

CONTENTS

SAVING OURSELVES FROM SUICIDE

BEFORE and AFTER

A Note to the Reader

F rom cover to cover, this is a life preserver. It's for everyone struggling with life challenges, hardships, or conditions such as depression and anxiety, as well as for those grieving through the aftermath of a significant loss. I wrote it with all of you in mind—for your family, your friends, and anyone else who cares about you. It's also for the people who want to lessen the pressure we put on ourselves, especially our youth, and live in a world with more kindness, empathy, and compassion.

The first half of this book is the true story of the heartbreaking life and suicide of Nick, my nineteen-year-old son. It also details the grief journey of the rest of my family—my husband, Tom, and my then seventeen-year-old daughter, Kelli. Using the insight gained from those experiences, I offer you helpful recommendations and practical advice in the second half, including many bulleted lists you can refer back to when needed. The real-life examples from my family's story give you solid takeaways to help yourself or the people in your life. For example, instead of merely giving a list of warning signs for suicide, I show you these signs in my son's behaviors and within his *actual* text messages, giving you a clear picture of what types of behaviors and communications to watch for in your family and friend groups.

Rather than simply supplying you with a list of recommendations for ways to work through grief, I allow you to witness my family's journey through it and see for yourself what worked for us, and what didn't. I describe in detail the bereavement journeys my husband, my daughter, and I had no choice but to take. I give you what helped us get through our grief, such as being kind and supportive to one another, training ourselves to turn negative thoughts into more positive ones, and relying on our faith. You will see how the three of us navigated our new family dynamic and what Tom and I had to consider when parenting our daughter after her brother's death. There were many steps the three of us had to take to get back into society after suffering such a profound loss. Learning what others feel and how they react when going through something similar to you can often provide comfort, knowing you are not alone in your feelings and actions.

You will read details about my son's suicide and the events leading up to his death, including bullying and other acts of unkindness. You will have access to personal and private conversations between my son and me about things like sexuality and fitting into society. I discuss many topics our society does not openly talk about and offer information you may find helpful for someone in your life. You will learn about the stigma that attached to Nick, before and after he died, as well as to my family. I tell how we have handled that stigma over the past seven years and discuss some common misconceptions about suicide.

As you read, consider the things Nick could not see, feel, or understand, like all the people who loved and cared about him, as evidenced by the testimonials at his memorial service. See the hope that was there for a good future and recognize the self-worth he was unable to understand or fully appreciate. Think about all the options he had, even though he thought there was only one—to end his life.

Hopefully, Nick's story inspires us all to find hope and see the people in our lives who care about us, that it helps us understand and appreciate our own precious value and the options we all have in life. Suicide is never the answer. There is no going back after making that choice, and there are no do-overs. I am sure Nick did not fully understand the finality of his decision or how it would shatter the lives of those he loved.

Rest assured, I'm not trying to be a psychologist or any other health-care professional. I don't think I have cornered the market on suicide or grief and make no claim to have all the answers. I'm a mom who loved her son wholeheartedly and unconditionally. Living with someone for nineteen years who was bullied, felt lonely, and ultimately suffered from depression that led to suicide has forever changed me and my family. My family has learned a lot being so close to Nick's pain, his needless death, and the aftermath as we navigated our grief. We did not understand Nick was suicidal and saw the warning signs only when it was too late. Benefit from our hindsight and everything else we learned through experience, research, conversations, and grace to help your loved ones, others around you, or perhaps even yourself.

Before my son died, I was busy with my life and unaware to what extent mental health issues exist in our world, let alone in my own home. Many of us live incognizant of them until someone we know and care about struggles to *stay* or, worse yet, leaves. Likewise, sometimes it takes a friend or loved one having difficulties fitting in or being treated poorly by others to open our eyes to the many people among us who are in pain. We suddenly see how necessary it is for us all to be more kind, accepting, and helpful to others, especially those in need.

As a society, we can no longer remain tight-lipped when it comes to mental health and suicide because there are too many people suffering. Those of us who have learned something about depression, anxiety, and other mental health issues need to share that knowledge to help those in pain and to offer information and assistance to families, friends, and everyone else who will listen. In this book, my family and I push away the stigma of mental health and suicide and hold nothing back.

This book would not be complete without addressing the pressure we put on ourselves and our young people, as well as the need for changes in our human interactions. I give suggestions about how we can lessen that pressure and share how we can create and implement a movement that calls for people to be more kind, compassionate, and empathetic.

As you read and gather tools to help yourself or someone else who may be hurting, keep in mind that this book is the inside view of just one story. There are many out there, and unfortunately, there will be many more to come if we don't start working together to lessen the pressure we put on ourselves and become a kinder and more compassionate world. Everyone, including government leaders, mental health professionals, parents, teachers, coaches, students, and clergy, must work together so we can accomplish these goals because mental health issues and suicide can happen to anyone and affect us all. We must all work together to be *Saving Ourselves from Suicide.*

In the past, where Nick saw no future, I can point others to hope and show options; where he felt sadness, I can bring comfort and give understanding; where he felt unkindness, I can inspire compassion and encourage inclusion; where our family missed warning signs, I can teach recognition and provide examples; where the world attached stigma, I can inspire sharing and model openness; where Nick and our family felt judged, I can lessen fear and point to truth; and finally, where my family experienced grief, I can suggest practical advice and offer recommendations.

—My version of the well-known Prayer of Saint Francis

Chapter 1

Losing a Child: A Metaphorical Look

On April 29, 2013, my kindhearted nineteen-year-old son, Nicolas, ended his life by jumping from a bridge into the Mississippi River just outside the University of Minnesota campus. Life as I knew it also ended on that day. He jumped very near a waterfall, so his body was unable to be found. A Minneapolis detective investigating Nick's death spoke to me later that day and said his body could churn in the waterfall for days, possibly never surfacing, and advised my husband and me to prepare for the worst. Getting that phone call every parent fears was difficult enough, but learning our son's death was a suicide and that his body might never be recovered was almost beyond comprehension. It was horrific.

It's incredible how the human spirit tries to cope with difficult news—even the most brutal. I tried my best to be okay with the idea of Nick's body being permanently lost in the Mississippi by telling myself he loved nature and now could be forever one with it. However, just as I started to wrap my brain around never getting it back, a Minnesota coroner called our home and told us his body had been found. It was almost four weeks since Nick had jumped.

I was relieved to hear that my son's body had finally been retrieved, but that relief suddenly changed to anguish as I began to think of him lying on some coroner's table. What condition was he in after being in the water for so long? My God, was he intact? Would the coroner treat his body with kindness and respect, or would my son be just one more John Doe with a toe tag to fill his workday? These questions and many more circled in my head and kept me up that night.

The next afternoon, that same coroner called back to say the body he thought was Nick's matched another young man's dental records—a high school student from Wisconsin who looked eerily similar to my son. The Wisconsin boy and his girlfriend made a suicide pact, drove across state lines to the Minneapolis bridges, and jumped just two weeks after Nick.[1] Four days after their deaths, a twenty-eight-year-old special education teacher jumped from yet another Minneapolis bridge.[2] At one point, Nick, the two Wisconsin teenagers, and the special education teacher were all in the Mississippi River, within the same vicinity . . . and four families lost their loved ones in the most unimaginable way.

Unless you have lost a child, it is difficult, if not impossible, to describe how much pain you feel. It is some of the worst emotional agony and suffering you can experience and still be alive. Imagine having open-heart surgery without anesthesia, and the surgeon removes a piece of your heart, creating a deep hole in your chest. Then, while you are lying on the operating table, instead of stitching you up, the doctor flips you a white cotton button-down shirt and tells you to get up, put it on, and go on with life as if nothing ever happened. You have a mortal wound, but you are expected to continue with your daily chores and tasks as if nothing ever happened.

On a pain scale of 1 to 10, it is 1,000, and because the thin, white fabric covers the hole from public view, no one knows the depth of your pain. Only those who care about you can see blood seeping through your shirt, yet even they cannot fully understand your pain or see the gaping wound that lies underneath. No matter how much time passes, this injury is not going away. The only thing that can make the pain disappear is to have someone put that missing piece back into your heart, but you know that is never going to happen—not in this lifetime.

As you try to get on with life, you often get what I call *pings* in this hole. Don't let the sound of the word *pings* fool you. It sounds like they would be little, wimpy feelings, but these pings are sharp, cutting pains. They happen when friends post pictures of their family on social media, saying how blessed they are for having everyone home for the holidays; when viewing people's photos of their kids graduating or getting married; when hearing songs on the radio reminding you of times spent together; or when spotting someone in a crowd who resembles your child or shares similar mannerisms.

Ping. Ping. Ping.

It's agonizing! Every day, and sometimes throughout the day, I still get these pings. All parents who have lost children do.

I am not jealous of others. I am genuinely happy for them when their kids do well or when they are united as a family in celebration, but that happiness is forever coupled with pain because I can no longer have that same joy with my son. The lives of my friends seem to be moving forward blissfully, while mine is going by more slowly because it is no longer carefree. Nothing in this world can fill the emptiness in mine.

Most happy moments in my family's future will be bittersweet. If my daughter gets married or has a baby, the joy we will feel that day will be tethered to sadness from Nick's absence in our celebration. These occasions will be reminders that my son will never enjoy the same milestones.

I imagine losing a child requires some of the same survival skills that recovering alcoholics need to function and thrive. Alcoholics have a lifelong addiction and must make a conscious choice every day to not give in to their illness or be defined by it, no matter how difficult life gets for them. However, with hard work and a lot of determination, they can live happy and productive lives while maintaining their sobriety.

Similarly, parents who have lost a child feel that loss throughout their lifetimes and must learn how to manage living with it—one day at a time. They have to push against their pain and choose to reach outward for the light, love, and joy in life while not letting their loss define them or take them down. With a strong will and daily effort, loss survivors absolutely can be happy again and lead fruitful lives. They eventually learn to accept that their hearts will never get that missing piece back under their white cotton button-down shirt. But they push on. Difficult days are inevitable, but they are still very much alive and have made it out of that operating room. With time, the support of family and friends, and a lot of self-determination, these parents eventually reach a point where good days far outweigh the bad, and they come to realize that living a happy, productive life is well within their grasp.

If you have lost a child and feel swallowed in darkness, hold on . . . and read on. Let me help you begin to find your way out of that dark hole of grief. If my husband and I, together with many other parents, could climb out, so can you. Don't lose hope because better days are ahead.

Chapter 2

Mental Health Issues and Suicide Can Happen in Any Family

have just described for you, metaphorically, what it is like to lose a child, but it was just a sketch. To get a better feel for it, you need more than that. You need to see a real-life portrait: one with a name, face, and family attached to it like the one I'm going to show you. With this particular portrait, you will take an up-close look at what it is like to lose a child and see how a somewhat hidden mental health concern led to suicide in a fairly typical family—my family.

This portrait is just one example of the many challenges our society faces today involving mental illness, like depression and anxiety, as well as the high occurrence of suicide that often results from such illness. But to have a real appreciation for how multifaceted and fast growing these challenges are, it is helpful to look at several portraits because each one differs from the next. We have much to learn and must do so quickly because the number of people in pain and struggling in our world is rapidly increasing, with far too many losing hope and choosing to end their suffering with a decision they can never take back.

So, what is a mental illness or mental disorder? (These two terms are often used interchangeably.)[1] The *Diagnostic and*

Statistical Manual of Mental Disorders (DSM-5), an authoritative guidebook used by mental health professionals and providers to make diagnoses of patients, defines a mental disorder as "a syndrome characterized by clinically significant disturbance in an individual's cognition, emotion, regulation, or behavior that reflects a dysfunction in the psychological, biological, or developmental processes underlying mental functioning."[2] This is a formal way of saying that mental disorders cover a broad range of mental health conditions that affect a person's thinking, mood, or behavior, causing difficulties in functioning.

We all have times when we feel a little down or experience the blues, but if ongoing symptoms rise to the level of impairing our daily functioning, then it may be more severe than a temporary glum mood and may very well be a mental illness.

It can be challenging to understand what is happening inside a person who has a mental disorder. No matter how hard I try, I cannot imagine the pain my son was experiencing or know how his brain was affected. Could he concentrate? Were his thoughts jumbled? Did he hear voices? Was he always anxious? Did he have some idea his mind was slipping?

Those who do not suffer from anxiety, depression, or any other mental illness need to try their best to be nonjudgmental, open-minded, and empathetic toward people who do. None of us can read a book or get a degree and believe we know exactly what a person suffering from a mental illness is going through. We must recognize we're limited because, ultimately, we are not the ones experiencing these issues.

Similarly, people who have not lived with or cared for someone with a mental illness often have difficulties understanding what family members and other caregivers go through. These individuals have an up-close look that fully involves them, yet they still feel like outsiders frustrated by trying to provide care without knowing precisely what the mental health sufferer is experiencing or feeling.

These caregivers often feel desperation, not knowing the best way to help, and ask themselves things like, "Should I insist he see a counselor, or will that make him angry? Should I mention that he seems to be having a difficult time holding down a job, or will that hurt his self-esteem? Should I ask him straight out if he is suicidal, or will that give him the idea?" They worry and pray, then worry some more. As a former member of this group, I can tell you . . . it is grueling.

To this day, many of my friends who never lived with anyone having mental health issues ask me questions to learn what Nick went through, and what Tom, Kelli, and I experienced before and after his passing. Some are just curious, but others want to learn more so they will know how to help their loved ones or friends if they begin to experience similar types of issues.

Answering questions can sometimes be difficult, more so in the past than now, but it is always good when people want to expand their knowledge and learn things like the risk factors and warning signs for suicide. Those of us who have had these experiences and are willing and able to open up need to share them with others. As a society, this is how we can learn more about mental health challenges. They are important to understand because, and I cannot stress this enough, they can happen to *anyone* in your life. Mental health issues and suicide do not care about your religious beliefs, political preferences, net worth, skin color, age, gender identification, sexual orientation, or anything else.

You may be thinking, "Those things can never happen in my family. Sure, we have our ups and downs, but no one in my family feels that bad or would do anything like that." Well, I believed the same things about my family. I admit the thought crossed my mind at one point during Nick's teenage years, which I will talk about later, but I had no idea he had a serious mental health problem—and never imagined he would *kill* himself. At times Nick could be a little awkward and had difficulties fitting in socially, but I didn't think he was suicidal. Toward the end of Nick's life, I knew he was depressed but believed it was a temporary condition brought on by outside factors, like being unhappy with his college choice and some inconsiderate, passive-aggressive young men at school. I figured he would be back to "normal" in a few weeks when he came home for summer break and his environment changed. Unfortunately, I had no idea his condition was as dangerous as it was and involved a life-threatening mental health component.

I learned a great deal from my son's life, illness, and death. Afterward, I talked with many families who lost loved ones to suicide, read suicide articles and attempt survivor stories, and attended many suicide prevention programs. I now understand that mental health issues and suicide can happen in any family—even yours. In fact, they can happen to anyone in your life: a spouse, child, niece, coworker, friend, classmate, employee, or neighbor. Any of the people you care about may be struggling and contemplating suicide right now, and you may be completely unaware.

The good news is that many suicides can be prevented. The following chapters provide ways we can focus on *Saving Ourselves from Suicide*, even ones that have already happened.

Chapter 3

Nick's Story

Nick was an extremely intelligent, loving, and compassionate young man. From the time he was a little boy, people often described him as being wise beyond his years, or an old soul. He had an intense passion for buildings and airplanes and would gladly share all he knew about them to anybody who would listen. Nick memorized facts about skyscrapers, aircraft, runways, and flight schedules and would light up every time he talked about any of them. Parents and teachers thought the world of Nick because he was so polite and passionate for someone so young, but kids his age had a difficult time relating to him. They neither appreciated nor understood his interests.

Nick had a big heart and started showing compassion from a very early age. In second grade, he befriended an Indian girl who was being shunned by her white classmates because they were too young to understand and appreciate her culture. Nick assured her it was good to be different because that made her interesting and encouraged her to embrace her uniqueness. He always tried to look out for those who felt left out.

If I had to describe Nick in three words, I would say he was pure, compassionate, and righteous. By righteous, I don't mean stubborn. Rather, he wanted to right the wrongs he saw in the world because they often upset him and weighed him down—sometimes to the point of crushing his spirit. If someone looked like he or she could use some help, Nick was happy to do whatever he could.

One time in high school, he overheard some underclassmen guys call their female classmate a whore. Nick didn't know the girl, but when he saw the group start closing in, he stood in front of her like a shield and told them to knock it off and leave. As she stood there crying, Nick put his arm around her and escorted her to some chairs in the school lobby where he consoled her until he felt sure she was going to be all right.

In the fall of his junior and senior years, he made a point to reach out and talk one-on-one with many of the incoming freshmen so they would feel comfortable as they began high school. It touches my heart that Nick's Indian friend from the second grade and many of those former freshmen students spoke at his memorial mass about what his kindness meant to them.

Even at a young age, Nick was sensitive to the feelings of adults. During parent-teacher conferences, his middle and high school teachers told us how Nick would occasionally give them little pep talks if they had a particularly stressful day or were frustrated with students for acting up in class. He assured them they were good teachers and encouraged them not to feel bad because tomorrow would be a better day for everyone. I remember his high school Spanish teacher shaking his head in near disbelief as he recounted how Nick looked out for him one day. He said something like, "What high school kid cares if a teacher is having a bad day?" These are just a few examples of the many ways Nick cared for others.

After Nick passed, people came up to me and told me story after story about how Nick helped them, or how he made them feel better. I always knew my son was kindhearted, but I never realized how many people, of all ages, he positively affected until after he died. I think Nick knew too well what it was like to feel bad, and if he saw others going through a tough time, he tried his best to let them know he cared.

Throughout his entire life, Nick had difficulties making friends. Growing up, he never really had a best friend: the one thing he wanted most in life. Day after day, the pain of never having a close friend to hang out with was almost crippling to him. He yearned for that type of camaraderie and could not understand why, no matter how hard he tried, he couldn't have it. Kids his age hardly ever reciprocated his desire to be their friend, so he always felt rejected. As a parent, it was both frustrating and heartbreaking to watch because I didn't have control over how others treated him.

Once Nick got into high school, I believe a handful of kids genuinely cared about him and considered themselves his friend; however, after being rejected by his peers for so many years, I'm not sure how much Nick was able to feel the full extent of any friendships. He had been treated unkindly and bullied on and off throughout his young life, and it took a toll on him. Rejection upon rejection stacked up and eventually buried his hope for having a lot of friends or a happy future. All the disappointment and pain he had experienced throughout his life had a cumulative effect, causing depression at the end.

THE BIG GIVEAWAY

Nick never told anyone he was thinking about ending his life. He was able to hold it together and act upbeat in front of outsiders—even his own family. The only time he did anything Tom and I saw as being a potential red flag for suicide was during the summer before his senior year in high school. One day I went into his bedroom to hang up some shirts and noticed a lot of his clothes were missing from his closet. We had always encouraged the kids to give to charity by going through their belongings about every six months and bagging whatever clothes and items they had out-grown or didn't want anymore. However, this time was different because an alarming amount was missing, and Nick had not left the bags for me to drop off at church as I had always done in the past. Instead, he hauled everything away himself without me knowing it. As I stood in his room with his closet door and my mouth wide open, I took a mental inventory of all the things that were missing. Even the cherished knickknacks he brought back as souvenirs from our most recent vacation were no longer proudly displayed around his room.

When Tom and I asked Nick about everything that was miss-ing, he said it felt good to give to others because he had too much, and it wasn't right to keep it all when people in need could use it. Knowing Nick was a generous soul, his explanation seemed some-what plausible. He was, after all, a compassionate kid who often acted altruistically, like playing the piano at a nearby nursing home and picking up litter while on vacation. He might have been telling the truth, but Tom and I could not get past the fact he gave away some of his most treasured belongings, such as one of his trumpets and an iPod.

Years ago, we had heard that giving away prized possessions was a common warning sign for suicide, so we had to get a few opinions from mental health professionals to determine whether Nick's big giveaway was an act of charity or a call for help. We needed experts to help us assess whether Nick required immediate care. Also, he had plans to go to college the following year, and we had to figure out if it would be safe to let him move away from home. Was that even a possibility now?

THE ASPERGER'S THEORY

Nick saw two psychologists who gave us two different professional opinions about his behavior. It turned out neither psychologist thought Nick was suicidal, and both thought he would be fine going away to school—even out of state. One of the two, however, thought Nick had Asperger's syndrome and was functioning at an extremely high level. In fact, Nick was the highest-functioning "Aspie kid" he had ever seen.

Interestingly, the other psychologist made no mention of Asperger's or any other disorder. (People are no longer diagnosed with Asperger's because that diagnosis has been removed from the *DSM–5*—that same manual of potential diagnoses used by mental health professionals that I mentioned earlier. People with symptoms of what used to be called "Asperger's" are now said to be on the "autism spectrum.")[1]

At that time, "high-functioning" Asperger's generally meant an ability to engage in certain activities and social interactions with very few noticeable symptoms.[2] This seemed to fit Nick because he barely showed any visible signs of any psychological disorder. Sometimes he was just "quirky." As a comparison, the character Sheldon Cooper on the popular television series *Big Bang Theory* and *Young Sheldon* is portrayed as having Asperger's, but I think Sheldon in both series acts much more eccentric and quirkier than Nick ever did.

The psychologist who thought Nick had Asperger's only told Tom his theory, not Nick. Having never heard of Asperger's, we read some books and were surprised that some of the typical "Aspie" characteristics, symptoms, and idiosyncrasies matched what we had seen in Nick from the time he was a little boy. For example, Nick never had a slight interest in things; it was always an intense passion. First, it was cars and trucks, followed by maps and weather, and then airplanes and buildings. When he was little, he had difficulties making eye contact, but that improved with time after he practiced looking people in the eyes.[3] Also, that psychologist thought Nick's way of walking could be stiff at times and told us that was another Aspie symptom.

Assuming the one psychologist was right, and Nick had Asperger's, his high functioning complicated matters because he "appeared" to fit in well with others, but in reality, he struggled in social environments. This is true for most high-functioning Aspie kids. Nick's struggles were not apparent because they were internal, so people just thought he could be slightly different or say things a little off-center at times. If someone threw Nick a zinger or teased him, he sometimes understood the joke; but other times, he took the words literally and personally, not as lighthearted ribbing. Consequently, he could react defensively, even sharply at times, turning kids off. And because Nick didn't look like he had any psychological disorder, they were less likely to cut him slack whenever he misinterpreted social cues.

Nick's high functioning was not the only thing that masked his Asperger's; he also had an IQ in the "highly gifted range."[4] Having such a high IQ, he often thought brilliantly, learned new information quickly, and talked very much on point, making it seem as though Nick had his act together and was advanced for someone his age, not someone who had a mental disorder. It was quite the dichotomy. He was a hard read because there was no consistency in his behavior. In many social situations, he appeared quirky and a little clueless, and other times he seemed capable of curing cancer and saving the world (well, you get the idea). Nick's issue was truly complex. I could understand how the two psychologists had differing opinions about whether he had Asperger's, especially in a clinical setting versus a social one. If they could have observed Nick among his peers, perhaps they would have both agreed he had it.

Most people had no idea just how much Nick struggled to read people and social cues, not even Tom and me. He often said things innocently and well-intentioned, but there were times when they came off awkwardly. Most of the time, this happened when Nick talked to peers as opposed to adults. He was often nervous talking to kids his age because he could not relate to them as well as he could to adults.

One time, Nick told a neighbor who went to his high school that she had beautiful legs. He was not flirting with her; he just thought her legs were pretty and that it would be kind to tell her so. The poor guy didn't have the slightest clue his comment was somewhat inappropriate and made her feel uncomfortable. The girl's father told Tom about Nick's social blunder soon afterward merely to give him the heads-up that it happened. Fortunately, he was our good friend who knew our son his entire life and understood Nick didn't mean any harm. He laughed it off as "Nick just being Nick," but Tom wanted it to be a teachable moment for Nick, so he casually mentioned it to him. He didn't make a big deal of it because he knew Nick would feel terrible about the whole misunderstanding—and he did. Nick had absolutely no clue how his compliment came off and was mortified when he learned how uncomfortable it made the girl feel.

The psychologist assured Tom that as Nick got older, he would adapt by teaching himself different ways to interpret cues and, with time, would become more proficient at it. He also believed Nick would assimilate better with his peers once he reached his early twenties because maturity differences tend to even out in young adulthood. At that age, his peers probably wouldn't consider Nick's adult interests unusual anymore and would likely start sharing in them.

After much thought, Tom and I decided it was best not to tell Nick about Asperger's because we hoped the psychologist was right and things would get better in a few years. Why tell him if there was a chance things could work themselves out? Also, maybe he didn't even have it. We knew our son; he would have worried himself sick over the thought of even potentially having Asperger's. Like every parent, we wanted our child to be happy and feel confident when he left home for school.

Tom and I wanted to play it safe, so we asked Nick to continue seeing a psychologist periodically until he was ready to leave for college the following year. We left it up to him to decide which one of the two he wanted to see. Nick fought us hard on this, but he finally gave in and agreed to see the counselor who thought he had Asperger's. Tom drove Nick to see him a handful of times, but it was like pulling teeth each week because Nick kept insisting he didn't need counseling. Then one afternoon, Nick came home from an office visit and said the one thing that would make any parents not send their kid back. He told us that during their session that day, he thought the psychologist was "hitting on him."

Nick was always honest and never manipulative; however, we had a gut feeling he was making up these accusations. It seemed he cleverly figured out the one way he could stop going to counseling while still having our full support. Tom and I had checked out that counselor before Nick ever saw him and thought he was a pretty good guy, not someone who would hit on his patients. Unfortunately, there was no way we could be 100 percent sure. If we were wrong, we would be sending Nick back to a predator—and behind closed doors. We just could not take that chance, so we erred on the side of caution, gave Nick the benefit of the doubt, and allowed him to stop seeing that counselor.

For many weeks afterward, we tried our best to get Nick to make an appointment with the other psychologist he had initially seen and even gave him the option to choose a new one, but he flat out refused all of it. No matter how much we tried, Nick was adamant about not wanting to see anyone. He told us over and over that he was fine and didn't need to talk with anyone.

Convincing people to get help when they do not think they have an issue or don't want to go is difficult, if not impossible. They can be involuntarily admitted for treatment if they are in danger of harming themselves or someone else; however, we did not believe this was the case right then. We seemed to have reached an impasse because we had been told by two psychologists that our son was not suicidal, and Nick himself was telling us he was feeling good and was excited to go away to college.

What were we supposed to say? We could not tell him, "Nick, you gave away a lot of your clothes, so we don't think you should go to college next year—end of story. We don't care that you are telling us you feel fine and that both psychologists think you're not suicidal—you have to stay home. Oh, and by the way, we are making you go see a counselor every week, even if you don't think you need one." If we had taken that position, it would have caused all kinds of difficulties, including lowering Nick's self-esteem.

Our son was telling us he was feeling good, so we took him at his word and believed what he told us because he had never lied to us in the past. We assumed he would have shared with us if he was having difficulties and wanted to talk with a counselor because we were a close family that opened up to each other all the time. Both psychologists agreed he was not suicidal and had given us the thumbs-up for Nick to attend an out-of-state college, so the following year, that is exactly what we allowed him to do.

We were trying our best to do the right thing and did not think it was right to hold Nick back from his dreams.

SOCIALIZING IN COLLEGE AND MORE ASPERGER'S

Nick was very excited to start his freshman year at the University of Minnesota, Carlson School of Management. Like most kids his age, Nick was thrilled to leave home and start his college experience. With almost one full year of academic credits, he was looking forward to a whole new beginning and was hopeful that this time he was going to make a lot of friends at school. Sadly though, it just didn't turn out that way for Nick. He suffered even more rejections, making his first year of college his last.

Just like in grade school, middle school, and high school, Nick had to deal with college kids sometimes saying hurtful things to his face and behind his back. One day Nick told me about a time when he was hanging with a group of his peers and was one of two guys named Nick. He overheard a girl in that group question his friend about which Nick he was talking about when referring to a past conversation. She asked if it was "cool Nick" or "awkward Nick." Nick's eyes welled up with tears as he shared that story with me, and it broke my heart.

When Tom and I realized Nick was still struggling socially, even in college, we decided it was time to teach him about Asperger's. We still weren't entirely sure he had it but believed he had the right to know that one of the psychologists thought he did, especially if he was still feeling different from others and not understanding why. If he did have Asperger's, we figured maybe he could learn how to better interact with his peers by teaching himself alternative ways to read social cues.

Tom and I sat down with Nick and just leveled with him. We explained the one psychologist's theory and then briefly described Asperger's in general terms. We told him the psychologists never reached a consensus and explained our concern about labeling him, especially since he was never formally diagnosed. We explained the other reasons why we didn't tell him about the disorder earlier, like being advised the symptoms could significantly improve with age. Then we gave him the books we had on the subject and encouraged him to read them if he wanted to learn more. The most heartbreaking part was telling him that some of the symptoms we read about seemed to match certain behaviors we saw in him from the time he was a child, such as his intense interests.

We believed this was the best approach because it was giving Nick information, not a label. He was almost nineteen and extremely intelligent, so we thought this wasn't too much to lay on him. Because he loved to research things and learn about different subjects, we figured he would dive in and immerse himself with this new information. We were right. Within a few weeks, he read most of the books we gave him, or at least parts of them, and occasionally would refer to himself as having Asperger's. He didn't make a big deal of it, nor did we.

That following semester in college, Nick just happened to sit next to another student in the cafeteria who had been diagnosed with Asperger's. They had a long, friendly conversation together over lunch, and afterward, Nick couldn't wait to call home and tell Tom all about it. Nick described how that young man had pronounced signs of Asperger's and insisted that since he was nothing like him, he now knew there was no way he had it. Tom suggested to Nick that he might just be functioning at a higher level than that kid, but Nick was adamant he didn't have Asperger's, so Tom didn't push the topic.

We will never know if Nick had Asperger's because he was never formally diagnosed with it, or with any other disorder, but Tom and I still think he probably did and agree he was extremely high functioning. It's just a shame we never heard of Asperger's until Nick was seventeen years old because if we had, we could have better understood Nick's idiosyncrasies years earlier and learned ways to help him interact socially, especially with his peers.

PRIVATE RESIDENCE (FIRST SEMESTER)

From the time Nick started college, he hung out with both male and female students in an independent, religious-affiliated house just off campus and very near a church. For the first half of the school year, Tom and I thought it was on campus and owned by the university but later learned it was privately owned.

Nick spent most of his first semester at this private residence and went there for some dinners, social events, and even a retreat. He liked many of the kids who hung out at the house and planned to live there his sophomore year. Some bizarre things started going on there, though.

Two older men who had graduated from the university years earlier were living at the house with four or five students. Those younger residents, and even the kids like Nick who hung out there, were expected to follow some strange social rules whereby they had to open up and share all their feelings with everyone at the house. Also, each person was assigned a peer sponsor. The leaders told them if they ever felt sexual urges about someone, they had to call their sponsor to "talk them down" from those feelings.

Nick was a righteous guy. There was no way he was ever going to stay silent about these bizarre expectations. Several times he spoke up and told the older house leaders, and anyone else who would listen, that their rules were abnormal. Nick tried to convince them that as friendships develop, people naturally share some things about themselves to whomever they feel closest; however, it was wrong for them to expect students to open up and share all their emotions—and with everyone at the house. Most importantly, Nick tried to get them to understand that assigning kids a sponsor to stifle sexual urges was disturbing.

When Nick came home at winter break, he filled us in about everything going on at that house and was relieved when Tom and I validated all his concerns about residing there the following year. We strongly urged him to stay away from that place because none of it sounded right. Nick told us we had nothing to worry about because he reached the same conclusion on his own, even before he came home for winter break.

APARTMENT LEASE AND DILEMMA (SECOND SEMESTER)

For the entire first semester Nick had invested all his time and energy trying to get to know all the kids who both lived and hung out at that private house, but now that residing there was no longer an option, he didn't know where he should live the following year. Nick did not get along with his current roommate in the dorms, so rooming with him for another year was also not an option. It was the end of December, and by November, most kids had already formed friend groups to move into apartments off campus. Nick was late getting into a group and was stressing over it.

After winter break, a nice guy who lived down the hall from him in the dorm noticed how worried Nick was about finding guys to live with sophomore year. He liked Nick and wanted to help him because he knew all he had gone through at that private residence during the first semester. This guy offered to drop out of an apartment lease he was about to sign with some guys from another religious group and let Nick take his place on the leasing contract. Nick didn't know any of those young men but figured they must be nice if his friend liked them.

Nick was excited to make plans to live off campus and get to know this new group of guys. They met a few times, and he thought all was good, but every time he tried to get them to go to the leasing company to sign the lease, they made up some excuse. This happened numerous times, and they kept telling him they needed to get to know him better. During our weekly calls, we sensed Nick was very frustrated and stressed out over them not wanting to meet with him or sign the lease right away.

By mid- to late February, they still had not signed, so Tom advised Nick to play it safe and make a plan B. He encouraged him to sign up for a roommate and a dorm room through university housing just in case his plans fell through for the apartment. Nick did that and was assigned a roommate for the following year, a nice guy named Len. Nick reached out to him right away, and they hit it off and even hung out a few times toward the end of the second semester. I think Nick and Len would have gotten along well if they had lived together sophomore year because they seemed to have a lot in common and were both kindhearted young men.

Nick had a bit of a dilemma now. Len was lined up to be his roommate in the dorms, but Nick still had plans to live off campus with the guys who were stringing him along. Why didn't our son just pass on that group and stick to rooming with Len for his second year? Nick had conflicts with his freshman roommate all year, so you would think he would have jumped at the chance to live with someone he got along with for the upcoming year. Rooming with Len sure seemed like the obvious choice to Tom and me; however, many college freshmen would give up anything and everything for the opportunity to move off campus and live in an apartment. Unfortunately, Nick was no exception.

Over spring break, Nick told me he felt guilty that Len had no idea he still was trying to lease an apartment with those other guys. Ordinarily, Nick would have never treated a person like that, but he desperately needed his plan B. Although keeping both options open was the safest bet, he knew it was not the nicest—and Nick was a good guy down to his core.

It didn't surprise me when Nick decided a few days later to follow his conscience and tell Len about the apartment lease. Even though this meant possibly having no place to live sophomore year if his plans to live off campus failed and Len found a new roommate, Nick didn't have the heart to string Len along like the other guys were doing to him. He wanted Len to be able to find another person to live with before it got too late in the year to match with someone who still might be available. I was proud of my son because even though he was panicked about where he was going to live the following year, he didn't succumb to the pressure by acting selfishly and unkindly.

In mid-April, the apartment guys still had not signed the lease and even kicked up their stalling tactics by beginning to avoid Nick. One evening, Nick asked them to meet him for dinner in the cafeteria so he could flush out why they had been delaying for so long. The school year was soon coming to an end, and Nick wanted a resolution. Once again, they made up an excuse about why they couldn't meet with him, so Nick went alone to the cafeteria to eat dinner that night, as he did so often. As Nick walked through the cafeteria with his food tray, he ran into them sitting as a group toward the back of the cafeteria, where they must have thought he would never look. Nick chose not to approach them but called home right away to tell us how betrayed he felt. He was hurt that none of them had the decency, or respected him enough, to just say they didn't want to live with him.

Nick finally gave up. He decided it was best to just say he changed his mind about living off campus and wanted another year in the dorms. Being strung along for so long was one more painful rejection to Nick—one that lasted months and caused a great deal of stress and heartache. It was bad enough Nick was exposed to some weird stuff in that independent residence almost the entire first semester, but then having this additional major stressor throughout the whole second semester was just too much for him. At this point, Nick had gone through many school years of peers treating him unkindly. It didn't improve in middle school as he had hoped, it didn't improve in high school as he had hoped, and now it looked like it wasn't going to improve in college—in Nick's eyes, he was almost out of hope.

What Nick didn't realize, though, was that there was still hope in his college years. Yes, some of his peers treated him very unkindly—downright cruelly—but there were other people on campus who were kind and either wanted to be Nick's friend or already considered themselves to be his friend. Len still had not found anyone else to room with for sophomore year and was happy Nick once again asked him to room together. Tom and I know Nick also had a few friends from his business classes and a couple of others from the independent residence where he spent most of his time first semester, although we don't know if those friendships were close.

We do know for sure he had two good friends, Alex and Jerry. Nick would sometimes grab meals at the cafeteria, go off campus to catch a movie, or just hang out with them, one at a time. Nick and Jerry often worked out at the gym together. This should have been a happy ending to a tumultuous first year at college. Nick was set to start his sophomore year with a few kind friends and a new roommate who was quickly becoming another good friend. Unfortunately, the problems of freshman year were not over yet.

THE RUMOR

Fast-forward about three weeks. It was now two weeks before the end of the spring semester, and the students were having their last few classes before the start of final exams. Saturday morning at 6:20 a.m. on April 27, 2013, Nick texted me:

> Mom, I just had the worst day of my life yesterday. I need to call you right when I get off of work at probably 11. Please don't let this scare you. I'm managing but have had a few embarrassing and tough realizations to swallow lately. I'm trying to fight depression with all my might and don't know if I can stay here anymore. I'm doing my best. I'm studying. And I can't wait to go home.

I was still sleeping when I received his text. Seven minutes later, Nick texted again:

> Basically, I'm starting to see how much stuff I've been left out of by people I thought were my friends. They've been trying to hide so much from me. And I finally got a glimpse why. And now it makes so much sense.

I don't think it was a coincidence that I happened to wake up minutes later and turn on my phone. I saw Nick's texts and was frightened when I saw the word *depression*. The first time Nick ever mentioned feeling depressed was in a text message to me eight days earlier.

The following is an excerpt from that previous text conversation that occurred on April 19:

Nick

> It's just so hard . . . it seems like everyone leaves me out. I don't know why, and it really depresses me.

Linda

> What happened today sweetie?

Nick

> I'm losing my old friends and can't make any close new ones. People are polite but leave me out of things. I give up.

Linda

> Honey, I think people are busy on a merry-go-round and just busy going around and round. They aren't stopping you from getting on, they just aren't thinking about it. You have been so hurt by people in the past that you see them not stopping the merry go round for you as rejection. I think they aren't even thinking that way. I really don't think it's anything personal toward you. Really. They are just busy spinning around and around.

Nick

> Either way, it's pretty cold. It's like no one cares. And it's taking its toll.

Linda

> I think people care about you . . . I think other than your roommate, people generally really like you.

Nick

> He's gotten a lot nicer. I think I have too.

Linda

You have been so hurt in the past, I think you are sensitive . . . There's nothing wrong with you Nick. There's no reason to reject you. Are you thinking about Purdue still? If you need to talk to someone just to get it off your chest, go see someone at Boynton [the health center on campus where they have counseling]. I'm not saying I think you need it by any means. I'm just saying the service is there if you need it.

Nick

Mom no. I'm almost done with school.

Linda

Ok. Do you want to go back to Minnesota or Purdue?

Nick

I don't know but I'm struggling.

Linda

Are you going to be ok? How bad is it?

Nick

I'll survive. I'm just trying to study.

Linda

If it ever gets too bad, promise me you'll reach out to me. I know you are hurting, and I wish I could take it away. I wish I was there to give you a hug. I pray for you all the time.

Nick

I'm sick of complaining about it. I want to be upbeat.

Linda

You need to vent at times so do so to me. I'm your mom so do so to me. I think you are down to 4 weeks before the dorms close. Yeah!

Nick

Why has it been so hard?

Linda

I wish I had the answer. You are a terrific person Nick.

Nick

Thanks, I try.

Linda

> With pain there is much personal growth.

Nick

> I'm going to focus on the positive. There is still a lot to be thankful for. And I have to focus on school. How are you guys?

The next morning after the text conversation on April 19, Nick texted back:

> Thanks for talking to me yesterday. I'm doing better today. I've been studying, but a few people invited me to hang out last night.

When Nick first mentioned being depressed on the nineteenth, I was concerned, but I didn't think it warranted pulling him out of school or anything extreme like that because he was going to be home for summer break in a month. In hindsight, what Nick said in that conversation raised some red flags calling for immediate action, but I just didn't know any better at that time. Although I was trying to be a supportive and loving mom, there are many things I would have said and done differently after learning more about depression. (I share more about this in chapter 16.) Now it was eight days later, and this was the second time Nick mentioned he was depressed. He was hurting and wanted to talk to his mom.

I woke up around 6:45 a.m. and responded to him as soon as I saw his two texts. Because Nick said he would call around 11 a.m. when he got off work, I assumed we could not discuss this by phone right then, so I immediately texted him that if it got unbearable on the floor, he should go to the hotel on campus and get a room. I made sure he knew he could stay in that hotel room for the entire last two weeks of school, if necessary. Then I told him he was a wonderful son, and I loved him very much.

After Nick got out of the shower, he texted back and said he was going to look for a place where he could call me in privacy. A few minutes later he called me from a stairwell and said he was okay but couldn't talk because he had to go to his student job on campus. He promised to call me as soon as he got off work.

Nick was a tour guide for the admissions office at the University of Minnesota and absolutely loved talking with prospective students and their parents because it was an excellent way to share his knowledge about the university and give the high school kids some advice. He loved the job and considered it to be almost like a ministry.

After Nick died, the president of the university wrote me a letter and shared that several parents sent letters to the admissions office throughout that school year in gratitude for how kind Nick was to their children while he gave them campus tours. The president told me these parents specifically mentioned Nick by name, and he thought I should know about it because it was unusual for the university to get feedback like that about any one tour guide.

Nick wound up not working his entire shift that day because the people at the admissions office must have noticed something was bothering him and let him leave early. He called me as soon as he returned to his dorm, and we jumped back into our conversation right where we had left off. Nick told me someone on his floor had spread a rumor that he was gay. Some guys were laughing about it and making fun of him. He asked me with such pain and brokenness in his voice, "How can anyone be so mean?"

For the past few years, Nick had questioned his sexual orientation (who he was attracted to) and struggled with whether he was gay, straight, or asexual (experiencing little or no sexual attraction to others and/or lack of interest in sexual relationships or behavior). This was a personal, internal struggle that he shared only with me, Tom, and Kelli. Nick was confused and frustrated because he never felt a sexual attraction to either females or males. He didn't really understand asexuality. None of us entirely did. I think Nick just assumed he was gay because he wasn't sexually attracted to females but was confused because he wasn't attracted to men either. In hindsight, our family thinks this explains why some days Nick would say he thought he was gay and then other days that he was straight. He didn't know where he fit in life.

Not knowing his sexual orientation was tearing Nick up inside. Tom and I assured him that many teenagers question their orientation and suggested it might be as simple as having a low sex drive. We explained that sexual orientation could be confusing at times and difficult to figure out, especially as a teenager because of young age and changing hormone levels, but it would most likely become more evident over time. Years later, Tom and I learned that having no sexual desires is not due to a hormone imbalance, although some asexual people may have some hormonal issues just like everyone else.

In the past, Tom, Kelli, and I had assured Nick we would accept him for who he was, no matter his sexual orientation, because we loved him and just wanted him to be happy. He was grateful for our understanding and support and knew our extended family would be nonjudgmental and accepting as well because we had all talked about these things at holiday and birthday gatherings. We are a reasonably open-minded family and pretty much on the same page on most social and political issues.

Nick said the rumor was spreading like wildfire among the guys on his floor, many of whom were friends with his roommate. He tried to clear things up by talking to them about the rumor, but it didn't help. A few seemed to feel bad about laughing at him, but it was all still a big mess and out of control.

From the start of the school year, those guys were a reasonably tight group because many of them loved to get together and play computer games and smoke pot. Nick said they considered him an outsider because he never used drugs and didn't play many computer games. Flight Simulator was the only game he had ever enjoyed, but he had not played it much past middle school.

Nick and his freshman roommate were opposites (unlike Len, his lined-up roommate for sophomore year). Nick told me they argued a lot because his roommate had fellow gamers in their room almost every weeknight playing on the computer. They were loud and often kept Nick up into the early hours of the morning. Over time, this wore on Nick because he had to get up for his early morning classes. They also argued over the cleanliness of their room. All in all, their arguments seemed somewhat typical for first-year students, but things seemed to have escalated between them by year's end.

Now, after a long year of late nights, Nick was looking forward to the school year coming to a close. It was the last few weeks before the summer break. Nick almost made it to the end of the year, but then someone spread the rumor. The timing of it had the potential to do maximum damage because Nick had no way to clear things up before school ended. For the entire three months of break, Nick would agonize knowing his peers thought he was gay when he wasn't even sure about it himself.

Nick's sexuality was nobody's business. His internal struggle was private, not something to make fun of or laugh about. I couldn't believe my son was getting bullied in *college*. We didn't know for sure who started the rumor, but who initiated it was not as important as what was said. Gossiping about someone's sexuality is bullying—at any age.

After Nick and I talked on the phone awhile, I told him I had to hang up to jump in the shower because his father, sister, and I were going to a family celebration for his cousin. We agreed to stay in touch throughout the day.

All afternoon I talked with Nick on and off to get updates and assess how he was doing. During the car ride home from our family luncheon, Nick told me he thought he heard someone on his floor ask which guy was spreading the rumor. It sounded like maybe the rumor was getting out of control, and perhaps some of the young men were trying to do a little damage control.

At one point in our conversation, I straight out asked Nick, "Do you want me to come there and be with you?" There was a brief silence on the phone as he thought. My son never wanted to draw attention to himself and always had a difficult time reaching out and asking for help, but this time, he quietly said, "Yes." Then he added, "I've never been so appreciative of family." That was something he repeated a few more times that day and many times throughout that last weekend. When I hung up, I told Tom I absolutely had to get on the next flight to Minneapolis and be with Nick because he sounded so broken. Tom realized this was serious by the urgency in my voice and because Nick had asked me to fly out. He agreed that I should immediately go be with Nick.

As soon as we got home, Tom booked my flight and called Nick to tell him he was reserving a hotel room on campus. He encouraged him to stay there away from the guys who were giving him such a hard time. Tom even offered to book that hotel room until the end of the school year, which was just two weeks away. Meanwhile, I frantically packed a bag to leave.

Being like many women who do not travel for a living, I cannot pack quickly or lightly—ever. But like any mom with a child in need, that day I not only power-packed but would have moved a mountain if Nick asked, all while multitasking. It is an unwritten Law of the Universe: women become warriors when their kids need them. I'm not exactly sure how much time passed, but within less than an hour, Tom and I piled back into the car and made a mad dash to Midway Airport to catch the next flight out to Minneapolis.

THE FLIGHT

It was late Saturday afternoon, and traffic was building. What followed was another unwritten Law of the Universe: because we were in a hurry and running late for my flight, we caught way more than our fair share of red lights and even got stopped by a freight train. It was like there was some invisible force working against me making that trip. I fought hard to hold back my tears and texted Nick to tell him I was on my way but was probably going to miss that flight. I assured him if I did, I would definitely be on the very next one.

When I finally reached the airport, I had about nine minutes to board the plane before takeoff, including going through security. I got out of the car and ran like I was fleeing from gunfire. Somehow, I managed to get through security in just a few minutes, which any post-9/11 traveler would tell you was an absolute miracle. I pleaded with the female TSA officers to help me make my flight, while nervously explaining how I had to reach my son, who was being bullied. No doubt some of them were moms and could relate because when they heard this, they actually hurried. One of them even cheered me on as I grabbed my bags off the conveyor belt leading out of the surveillance detectors.

As I sprinted to my gate, all I could think was that it better be close because I had very little time and, at age fifty-one, even less endurance. Just when I ran out of breath and could not run anymore, I looked up and saw an airline employee at the gate closing the jetway door. I yelled for her to stop, and she held the door open for me as I ran past her and down the ramp gasping for air. My last step was an actual leap onto the plane grazing the flight attendant standing there preparing for takeoff. She immediately reached behind me and locked the plane door as I burst into tears and let out a big sigh of relief. She asked me if I was okay, and I gave her a quick nod and walked to my seat wiping my eyes while trying not to look at the other passengers staring up at me from their seats.

I took my phone out to text Nick before takeoff to tell him I made the flight. "Your mom is face. I made it." It was supposed to be, "Your mom is fast," but I was shook up. Nick responded, "Woohoo!" That one exclamation comforted me because I knew he was happy, even if it was just for that moment.

I had to turn my phone off for takeoff, so we had to end the conversation there. I spent the entire flight anticipating what Nick might tell me and thought about what I could say or do to help him feel better. From the time Nick was a little boy, I could always cheer him up after our talks, but this time seemed different. I was scared.

SATURDAY AND SUNDAY

It was just after 9:30 p.m. when I finally reached the hotel on campus. I texted Nick from the lobby to tell him I had arrived and suggested he leave a note for his roommate letting him know he was going to be away for a few days so no one on his floor would worry if they noticed he was not around. At the end of our two-week hotel stay, we could fly home together after finals and drive back to Minnesota to pick up everything from his dorm room.

We spent Saturday night, Sunday, and Monday morning talking together. We talked more about the rumor, and Nick shared how much it hurt whenever the guys on his floor would get together and exclude him, like when they would go to the cafeteria for a meal. They'd walk into his room and ask his roommate to join them and act like Nick was not even there. He said, "Mom, you think one of them would say, 'Hey, Nick, do you want to go with us?' They sometimes treat me like I'm invisible." Nick felt they would never like him because he didn't smoke pot or play computer games, so he had to go to other places for friendships. That's why he spent most of his time trying to get to know the kids in that private residence off campus.

As Nick opened up to me, I did my best to comfort him by telling him how sorry I was that he was going through all this. My heart broke as I listened to him, and I wanted to say that in ten years this stuff wouldn't matter; however, it very much mattered to him now and was causing him great pain.

We talked and talked—then even talked some more. He seemed to feel better as the weekend went on and was able to get a lot of things off his chest. We agreed it would be best if I laid low in the hotel room while I was there because we didn't want any of the guys from his floor to see me on campus. They would surely make fun of him for having his mom fly all the way from Illinois to be with him. If they were already saying terrible things, I could just imagine how they would react to Nick's "mommy" coming to "rescue him." Sunday night we even skipped going to church just off campus so no one would see me. I wish now we had gone that weekend, especially since it turned out to be the last chance for Nick to go, but I was just trying to do the right thing and keep him separated from anyone causing him grief.

We talked for hours on end, and I even got him to smile and laugh a little that weekend. Over and over, he expressed how much he appreciated me being there to help him and how grateful he was for having the support of his family. Nick was such a gentle soul. How could anyone want to hurt him? And how could something so terrible be happening to someone so sweet? On Sunday night before I fell asleep, I prayed hard for Nick. I asked God to put extra angels on Nick because he was so vulnerable at this time. I have no doubt they were with him as his life was coming to an end.

FINAL MORNING

The next morning, Tom called my cell phone to check on Nick and hear how he was doing. We told Nick again that he could stay in the hotel room with me for the next two weeks and study for his exams in peace. He thought about our offer for a few seconds and told me I should probably book a flight home on Tuesday, the next day, because he was feeling better. He did seem more at ease, but Tom and I weren't comfortable with me leaving him quite yet. We thought it would be best for me to stay through Thursday, at the very least, to make sure Nick was going to be all right. Since Nick was finally feeling better, I didn't want to have a disagreement with him about staying longer and figured we could talk about it when he returned to the hotel room after class.

Tom asked me to put Nick on the phone one more time, and he told him how much he loved him. They spoke about how Nick was feeling, and Tom assured him that everything was going to be all right, although Nick didn't seem convinced. He asked, "But what if I'm gay?" Tom told him he could have a happy life no matter his sexual orientation, and then they discussed how gay marriage was soon going to be legal. Tom even mentioned how Nick could adopt kids someday if he wished. Then Nick said his last words to Tom, "I love you, Dad."

It was around 10:30 a.m. when we hung up with Tom. Nick had a philosophy class at 11:15 a.m., and I was going to walk to a nearby restaurant to order carryout food and bring it back for him to eat before class. I asked Nick what he wanted for lunch. Shaking his head and shrugging, Nick let out a big sigh. "It really doesn't matter."

I remember thinking that response was a little strange but thought he was just tired from everything he had been dealing with that weekend. I asked him again. This time he told me to get him something with chicken in it, like a taco or burrito, but said it in a way that made me think he was appeasing me.

While I was gone, Nick wrote out a little schedule for the day on hotel stationery, which showed he would be out of the hotel room and on campus from just after lunch until early evening. He was going directly to class, to tutoring, to work out, and finally to eat dinner in the dining hall before returning to the hotel room. I think Nick purposely made this schedule showing he would be busy all afternoon until early evening so I wouldn't worry when he didn't come back to the hotel room in the afternoon and go out looking for him. Nick was giving himself time to take his life.

I brought the takeout food back to our hotel room, and we had what turned out to be our last meal together. As Nick quickly ate his food, we continued talking about the things he and Tom had spoken about earlier—how he could get married and have kids even if he was gay. We also discussed how he would be "Uncle Nick" to Kelli's kids someday. We laughed at the thought of Kelli having a ton of children and how one of them would always be visiting him, never allowing him a day to himself. I told him he didn't have to worry about marriage and kids right now.

Nick mentioned he was going to stop at Jamba Juice on campus right before class to get his friend a gift card for her birthday. I firmly suggested, like moms do, that he wait to do that after class because he was running short on time before his 11:15 a.m. class. After Nick ate his lunch, he started to consume several of the granola bars I had bought him on Sunday. One after another, he stood there and ate almost the entire box. This too was a little weird, but I thought maybe he was just hungry. He was, after all, a teenage boy. In hindsight, knowing Nick did not like to waste, I think he ate all those bars knowing I would have had to throw them out after he died because I was gluten-free and could not consume any of them.

When he left for class around 11:00 a.m., I remember the exact words we said to one another as I hugged him goodbye. "Nick, I love you. I'm proud of you. And you're so strong." He hugged me back. "I love you, too. And you're right, I am strong." Then Nick walked down the hallway toward the elevators with a big smile on his face and, literally, a hop in his step.

JAMBA JUICE

I straightened up the hotel room for about a half hour and decided to go to Jamba Juice to surprise Nick and get him his own gift card so he could have a smoothie anytime he wanted while studying for finals. It was a beautiful, sunny day in late April and people were walking around in light jackets with a look of relief on their faces after a long, hard Minnesota winter. As I walked into Jamba Juice, I saw something I did not quite understand. It was Nick . . . but how could that be since he left for class a half hour ago? He was bent over the front counter frantically urging the girl at the register to look at his driver's license and school ID. I could tell by the desperate tone in his voice that he was upset—not angry but panicky. He moved his IDs closer and closer to the girl while pleading, "Here, here . . . here are my IDs. Oh my gosh, you think I'm stalking you? I'm not stalking you! Here, go ahead and look at them!"

Nick was desperately offering them to assure the girl she was safe, and he was innocent with nothing to hide. She looked startled. Her eyes got big as she held out her arms and waved her hands quickly from side to side gesturing that she didn't need or want to look at his IDs, while repeating over and over, "No, no, no . . . I don't think you're stalking me. I don't think you're stalking me." Neither of them noticed me standing behind them. It appeared to be some big misunderstanding—and all on Nick's side.

I intervened. "Nick, it's okay! She doesn't think you're stalking her. It's okay." Nick turned around and with a confused look asked me what I was doing there. I told him I wanted to surprise him with a gift card of his very own. Then I tried my best to assure him it was all just a big misunderstanding. Suddenly, I realized the time and reminded him he was about twenty minutes late for class. I thought I was doing the right thing by making sure he didn't miss more class time because it was the last few weeks of school when professors usually give essential instructions about their finals. I told Nick I would stay behind and make sure everything was okay.

As Nick walked toward the door, he stopped, looked back at me, and paused. He was taking in the sight of his mom one last time. The sun coming in from the storefront window and glass door behind him was so intense, I could only make out his silhouette. The bright sunlight eerily created a halo that radiated all around him.

I had never seen Nick as upset as he was during that exchange at the counter. I was sick at heart with concern, but instead of grabbing him and making sure he was okay, I went to the wrong person—the girl. I wanted her to tell me the backstory to the misunderstanding so I could better help Nick comprehend it once he returned to the hotel room. I thought he could make it through class, even though he was still somewhat upset when he left. This would be the biggest mistake of my life. It all happened so quickly. In about two minutes from the time I first walked through the door, Nick was gone forever. I would never see my sweet boy again. Why didn't I hug him and talk with him right there? I will regret not doing so for the rest of my life, but there are no do-overs with suicide. It doesn't matter that I was well-intentioned that day.

As soon as Nick left, I tried to find out what happened. "What was that all about? Did you think my son was stalking you?"

"Noooo," the girl said, visibly shaken over the incident.

I told her he was my son and was one of the kindest people in the entire world. I assured her he would *never* stalk anyone. She said she knew that because he had come in to get smoothies now and then, and they got to know each other a little. She explained how they would see one another around campus and often wound up studying in the same place, although they never sat together. They didn't know each other that well yet.

She told me he came in today and ordered a gift card, and while she was ringing him up, he commented on how he recently saw her studying in a different place than she usually did. She told me she jokingly asked him, "What, are you my stalker now?" Then she smiled in a way that made it clear to me . . . she wasn't accusing him of anything; she was just *flirting* with him! Poor Nick failed to pick up on her "social cue" and was oblivious. The girl guessed he must have gone to class and felt so bad thinking she thought he was stalking her that he walked out of his lecture and returned to the store ten to fifteen minutes later to clear things up. This poor girl felt sick about the misunderstanding and explained to me, once again, how she was just joking with him. I told her it was all right, and I would make sure he understood that she didn't think he was stalking her.

But it wasn't all right. I was alarmed by what I had just witnessed. I called Tom while I was still in Jamba Juice out of the girl's earshot and told him we had to get Nick home right away because I had just seen something in him that scared me. I explained what happened, and he agreed. He even thought Nick might be so embarrassed by the exchange, and by me witnessing it, that he wouldn't want to return to the hotel room. At first, I thought Tom was overreacting, but then I got a sick feeling and wondered if he might be right.

THE WAIT

I went back to the hotel and just sat and worried with my stomach in knots. I turned on the television to quiet my mind, and *The Incredible Hulk* movie was on. I watched it with my eyes, but my mind was too deep in worry to focus. I sat there anyway and tried to take it in because it was the best way I knew to pass the time. At some point, I gave up and decided to go for a quick walk around campus.

It was an exceptionally bright day. I noticed the students all looked very serious as they quickly walked past me, probably because finals were only a few weeks away. As I walked, I worried with anticipation about Nick's return to the room and tried to think of what I could say to comfort him. Something in Nick showed through while he was in that Jamba Juice, and I wondered what it was. It frightened me because I had never seen it before. My mind kept racing, and I realized I needed to get back to the room just in case he decided to cut his schedule short and return to talk with me.

As I slid my keycard in the door, my cell phone rang. It was my daughter, Kelli, back in Illinois. She had just come home from school when a Minneapolis detective called our home phone looking for me. Not letting it go to the answering machine, a rarity for any teenager, she picked up and told him I was visiting Nick in Minneapolis. She gave him my cell number and then called me to give me the heads-up. Understandably, she was anxious. I quickly explained to her how I had not heard from Nick since he left for class, and that he was around campus doing things but would be returning to the room after dinner. We hung up right away so the detective could reach me. My stomach tightened as I braced for bad news. From that point on, it was a little like having an out-of-body experience.

Within a minute or so, the detective called my cell. After introducing himself, he asked when I had last seen Nick, and I told him sometime between 11:30 a.m. and 12:00 noon when he left to go back to class. He said he found Nick's backpack by a bridge in Minneapolis just off campus. Nick once told Tom he liked to study in an area below one of the bridges because it was so peaceful there, so I shared that information with the detective and suggested maybe Nick was doing homework or walking around that area. In hindsight, Tom and I wonder if Nick was dangerously comforted by the sight of that bridge because he may have considered it his exit plan if he ever felt like he couldn't go on.

Sure, I wish I had known how close that bridge and the other bridges were to campus, and the history of people jumping from them; however, I can't feel remorse about what I didn't know or couldn't predict. None of us can discover every single danger posing a threat to our loved ones. If like me, you did not foresee the lethal means used by your loved one, you must not blame yourself for his or her attempt or suicide. The suicide wasn't your fault. No one should ever carry that baggage around because it will *mess you up*. We are humans. Very few of us can predict the future. Please do not blame yourself.

The detective was concerned because there was a note by the backpack that appeared to be a suicide note signed by Nick. He had spoken to a few witnesses who from a distance saw Nick standing on the bridge, as well as another witness who saw him in the water frantically swimming toward a massive, nearby waterfall. No one saw him jump. He warned me that eyewitness accounts were often inaccurate and unreliable when they involve tragedies. I tried hard to understand what he was telling me. He seemed to be saying he thought Nick jumped, but everything else might be speculation.

My heart sank, and at that moment, I knew Nick was gone. I felt it. The detective asked if he could come to my hotel room to talk. I agreed, hung up, and in a daze sat myself down on the floor with my back against the wall repeating over and over, "Nick, what did you *do*? What did you *dooo*?"

My mind darted back to Kelli who had to be anxiously waiting by her phone. I needed to call her back to tell her what happened. It was gut-wrenching telling my child that her brother died. Other than asking a few questions, Kelli was understandably quiet and told me she was going to ask a friend to come over to be with her. Tom was in his office in downtown Chicago, and I had to call him next.

Tom clung to the hope that Nick was still alive, although deep down inside I think he knew he wasn't. He told me to look for Nick because maybe he was injured and lying on a riverbank somewhere close to where he jumped. We talked about the waterfall, and I explained how deep inside my heart, I felt he was no longer alive. Call it maternal instinct, or whatever . . . I could not put it into words. I just *knew* he was gone and not lying somewhere hurt. The detective was making his way to the hotel room to talk with me, so I couldn't leave anyway.

Tom was going to catch the next train home to be with Kelli. I wondered how he was going to make it, having to be around a bunch of people on a train right after hearing his son died so horrifically. He later told me that in shock, he sat in the stairwell of the train car, away from the other passengers with his head in his hands, praying that somehow Nick might still be alive.

I was worried about Kelli because she was home alone, and I had just told her what had happened. I felt like I had to say something to her because when the detective first called our home, he had told her enough to get her panicked. In hindsight, I wish I would have just said the officer found Nick's backpack and was still looking for him. Then, when Tom got home and was able to be with her, we could have told her, together, about Nick's suicide. I just wasn't thinking straight from the shock of it all. I was having knee-jerk reactions and couldn't weigh things while looking at the bigger picture. Instead, I told her the truth. It was instinctual to be honest with her because we were a family that didn't keep anything from each other.

Very recently, Kelli shared with me that when the detective first called our home looking for me, he told her that Nick had jumped. She knew before me. The detective probably had no idea he was talking with a seventeen-year-old. When she hung up with him and called me, she didn't tell me what happened to Nick because she didn't know how to break it to me. What teenager would? So, for five years, I felt terrible for telling Kelli about Nick when she was home alone, learning years later, she had already known. And Kelli felt bad that whole time for not being the one to tell me.

VISIT FROM DETECTIVE

I sat still on the floor in the corner of the hotel room waiting for the detective. I never moved. It seemed like a long time before he finally arrived. After letting him in, I returned to my spot on the ground, sitting with my knees up and back against the wall. The floor was hard, and the wall was cold, but that wasn't enough to make me move. I was numb.

I told the detective why I was on campus visiting Nick— about his call to me on Saturday and about the rumor. I told him everything, including how Nick was a sweet guy and always had been throughout his life. Then we had the typical exchange you see on most police television shows. Did Nick ever do drugs? No. Do you have a picture of him? I forwarded one off my cell to him. Did Nick have any tattoos? No. Afterward, it hit me why he asked for his picture and about tattoos. It was for identification purposes to aid the coroner if his body would later be retrieved from the Mississippi.

Before the detective came to my room, he interviewed some of the witnesses on the bridge and questioned some of the guys on Nick's floor. That explained why it had taken him so long to come talk with me. He said in all the suicide cases he had ever worked, including those where people jumped into the Mississippi, most of the people had significant issues involving drugs or alcohol. He was surprised to learn from those who knew Nick that he was "a good kid and not into any bad stuff."

Since that day, I have thought several times about what that detective said. That statement may have been true from his personal experience; however, certainly not all suicide cases involve drugs and alcohol. And even when individuals have used substances before their suicide, I believe many of them were good people, too. They were just going through severe difficulties in their lives. Good people of all ages and all walks of life die from suicide.

My husband called my cell after he made it home to Kelli, and I put him on speakerphone so he could talk with me and the detective at the same time. The detective told us the waterfall that witnesses had seen Nick heading toward was extremely treacherous, and it was highly unlikely anyone, not even an Olympic swimmer, could survive going through it. He warned us that last year one body had gone in there and never came out, and several others had spent weeks churning in that same waterfall, so we needed to prepare ourselves that we may not get Nick's body for a while—and perhaps not at all. It was almost beyond human capabilities to absorb and process all this devastating news at once.

Before the detective left my hotel room, he asked if he could send a social worker to talk with me. I thanked him, but said no. I wanted to be left alone to process what just happened. After he went, I remember some administrative person from the University of Minnesota called my cell phone and offered to have one of the university's social workers come to the hotel and talk with me. I politely declined again, expressing my need for solitude.

I have no real concept of time after the detective left my room because everything was a blur at that point. I just sat in the same position on the floor with my back against the wall, looking out the window across the room. I watched it gradually get darker outside as the sun was setting. The room filled with shadows, but it wasn't worth mustering up the energy to get up to turn the lights on until darkness almost entirely enveloped the room. How was I ever going to find the strength to make calls to our extended family and closest friends to let them know Nick was gone?

Chapter 4

Calls, Dorm, and Trip Home

MAKING CALLS

The first call I made was to my mother, a spunky, strong-minded woman in her late seventies who adored her only grandson. Grandma and Nick had always played a game where they would compete to be the last one to say, "I Love You Most Infinity" before they said goodbye to one another, whether in person or on the phone. He was her "Pooky Bear," a nickname she called him from the time he was a baby.

Breaking the news to my mom was difficult, especially because she was a dialysis patient with diabetes and two stents in her heart. I worried she might have a stroke or heart attack when I told her the devastating news. How could I possibly tell my mother, whom I loved so much, that her only grandson just died? I just got done telling Tom that his son killed himself, and Kelli that her brother was gone. There was no end to the pain, and now it was spreading to everyone I loved most. I knew I had to be the one to tell my mother, so I took a few deep breaths, picked up the phone, and made the call.

My mom was always happy to hear from me. It didn't matter if she was in the middle of doing laundry, washing a floor, or getting ready to walk out the door. As soon as I said, "Hi Mom," she could tell by the tone of my voice that something was terribly wrong. When I told her, she was devastated, of course, but assured me she would be okay. As moms do, she immediately thought of my needs before her own and tried to be strong for me. That was Mom. She was one tough cookie and came out of the womb that way. The youngest of eight children born to Slovak emigrant parents, she survived my dad's indiscretions and a brutal divorce, while still managing to raise two teenagers by herself. I asked her to call some friends to come over and sit with her.

The next call I made was to my cousin Jim asking him to book a flight that night to help bring me home because I knew I couldn't do it on my own. I was broken and needed help. I'm usually almost pathologically unable to ask anyone for assistance—but not that day. Tom needed to stay home and comfort Kelli. Jim was like a brother and would do anything for me. Since his kids were grown, I knew there was a good chance he could drop everything and get to me that evening. I was in no condition to call the airlines, make travel arrangements, or travel home by myself. Even with Jim's help, I wondered how I was going to get through a busy airport and sit on a plane among a bunch of people I didn't know for an entire flight.

Next, I called my only sibling, Paul, and asked him to drive from the city to our mom's house in the far suburbs. I thought it was more important for him to stay with her and keep her safe than fly to Minneapolis and get me home. Although he, too, was badly shaken from the news, he kindly agreed to make the trip and stay with our mother.

I knew my closest family members would take care of calling the rest of our extended family. I made just two more calls, both to friends. Telling the people I loved so much that Nick had died, and especially how he had done it, was awful. With each call, I realized I was changing their lives and causing them great pain.

TRIP TO DORM

The University of Minnesota people called one more time to make sure I was okay. This time I told them I wanted to go to Nick's dorm room to get a few of his belongings to take home with me. They agreed to have someone meet me there, so we arranged a time, and I went. I don't remember what time that was, but it was dark outside. When I walked into the building, two people were waiting at the front desk for me. I think the man was the hall director for that dorm, and the young woman was the resident assistant of Nick's floor. They told me they were sorry for my loss and handed me a cardboard box. In silence, we walked upstairs together and down the hall to Nick's room.

I expected to see some of the guys on the floor who made fun of Nick that weekend, but no one was around. Maybe someone had told them I was coming, and they scattered. The hall director opened Nick's door. After thanking them, I went into the room by myself and closed the door behind me. I wanted privacy in case I broke down crying as I went through Nick's belongings, but immediately after I shut the door, the hall director and resident assistant opened it. They just stood there with their backs against the door and arms crossed on their chests staring at me, body-blocking me from closing the door again. They told me they couldn't let me be alone in the room because that would go against their "policy." I remember thinking, "What policy? This was a suicide. Are you saying you have a dorm policy for when kids from your halls die by suicide?" I wondered how often that happened.

There I was holding a cardboard box with two escorts, feeling like I just got fired from a major corporation. They were treating me like a disgruntled employee, not a grieving mother. Was it too much to ask to be alone in my recently deceased son's room so I could go through his possessions? What did they think I was going to do, reach into Nick's desk drawer, take out scissors, and demand that his floormates tell me why they hurt my son so much? Talk about cold . . . these two made me feel like I had done something wrong and could not be trusted. I had no energy to make a case for my privacy, so I just grabbed a hoodie out of Nick's closet that I knew my daughter would want for sentimental reasons, together with a few of his holy medals, and walked out of his room in defeat.

I asked the two human shields when the guys on the floor found out about Nick's suicide. They said they only told his roommate and a few young men in the adjacent rooms but were not going to inform the others Nick died. I shook my head in disbelief and said, "But he's not coming back, so they're going to wonder where he is." They had no response—none. Instead, they walked me down the hallway, back down the stairs, and escorted me out of the dormitory. I didn't think it was possible to hurt more, but these two made me feel worse.

TRIP BACK HOME

Eileen, my dear friend from back home, called when I got back to the hotel room. She was worried about me and asked if we could talk until my cousin Jim arrived, not caring how long that would be. I have no idea how long we spoke, or what I said in those hours, but I am forever grateful she stayed on the phone with me that night.

As soon as Jim arrived, I showed him a copy of Nick's suicide note the detective had left with me, and we talked about how it was so loving and kind. You could tell by the contents that Nick wrote it, or at least part of it, at the bridge. He wrote a loving message to Tom, Kelli, and me, which included touching words of gratitude for each of us. Nick thanked me for being such a supportive mom and said his soul was therefore at peace. He even took the time to say kind things to a few friends on campus. In the P.S. he told Grandma, "I Love You Most Infinity," and, believe it or not, added a smiley face because he knew that he was saying the final words for their ongoing game. Six months later, right before my mom's sister died, she asked my mom if she had any messages for Nick. Her eyes lit up, and with a huge grin she answered, "Yes, tell my Pooky Bear, 'I Love You Most Infinity.'"

Nick ended his note with a few comforting lines for the Jamba Juice girl. Knowing Nick, he was probably worried she would find out what happened and think she had something to do with it. He was always looking out for others, even to the end. My cousin Jim and I wondered how Nick could write a note that was so loving, thoughtful, and almost tranquil right before doing something so tragic. He wrote that although he knew we thought his life should go on, it was time for him to go.

I did not sleep that night because I kept thinking about Nick's last moments and that his body was floating in the dark Mississippi River, or worse yet, churning in that waterfall. I had to keep reminding myself that it was just his body in the water, and his spirit was now in heaven. I lay there reminiscing about when he was a baby and how much he loved taking a bath in his little tub that I'd place in the kitchen sink. Then when Kelli was about one and Nick was three, I started putting them in the regular bathtub together, and they would have a blast playing with tub toys while laughing and singing. Every bath they had me sing Dean Martin's "That's Amore" over and over. I knew only a few lyrics, so my version was pretty short and repetitive, but the kids still loved it. I lay in bed thinking of the cold, murky water Nick was in now, and it was almost too much to bear. I could not wait until sunrise when I could get up, keep myself moving, and not think so much.

Jim and I took a taxi to the airport the next morning. I kept myself somewhat together the whole ride until we passed a large bridge in the distance. The sight of it made me burst into tears, even though I didn't know for sure if that was the one. I sobbed. This was the first time I cried since it happened, so it was like opening the floodgates. Jim put his arm around me and told me to hang on, as I did deep breathing in the back of the taxi like I was in labor ready to give birth.

At the gate, I sat limp waiting to board, not knowing how I was going to make it through my flight. My cell phone rang. It was a family friend who told me her husband received a message from Nick in his dream the previous night. He tossed and turned the whole night as he dreamed the same thing over and over— that he was receiving a text on his cell phone from Nick that said, "I'm OK Nick :)." The dream was vivid and seemed so real that he got out of bed to check his cell phone, even though he knew Nick had just died. What her husband didn't know, however, was that Nick almost always ended his texts with a smiley face, not the emoji but the colon-and-parenthesis type, just like the one in his dream.

That smiley face in my friend's dream was too much of a coincidence for me not to consider it as a message from my son. It made perfect sense Nick would communicate through the husband because he knew him well and trusted him. Nick most likely understood Tom, Kelli, and I were in shock and not thinking straight from our grief. We had not slept, making it impossible for him to communicate in our dreams, and we were too much in a fog to pick up any signs or messages from him. Nick must have trusted that our friends would call me to relay the communication that he was okay. I do believe the dream was indeed a message from Nick, but even if it wasn't, hearing about it at that exact time gave me the strength I needed to board the plane and make my trip home.

FRONT LINE OF SUPPORT

My cousin Bill, Jim's brother, who is also like a sibling to me, picked us up at the airport and drove me home, where my close girlfriends were waiting to offer support. Two more Laws of the Universe: family takes care of family, and girlfriends take care of girlfriends. For the next few weeks, a steady stream of people came to offer condolences and talk. I was very open to this because I considered it an opportunity for us all to talk about what happened to Nick and share our faith.

It sounds like I had my act together, but I assure you I did not. You might wonder what changed. Why did I reject talking to anyone in Minneapolis but now welcome visitors? The difference was I knew the people at home—family and close friends offering loving support. I didn't know anyone in Minneapolis, and the whole time I was there, I just wanted to be left alone to absorb what happened. Now, I needed my family and close friends to help me heal. Talking about it was therapeutic because saying what happened over and over was helping me wrap my brain around what seemed so surreal.

Chapter 5

Initial Days of Grief

FIRST DAYS

Now that you know the particulars of how Nick died, I think it would be helpful to describe those initial days of our grief. In chapter 11, I talk about the grieving process throughout the crucial first year and how it changed over the following five years. If you too are grieving, our story may comfort you to learn you are not alone in experiencing a whole range of raw emotions. Or, if you are someone having a difficult time understanding what family members or friends are going through after their loss of someone, then learning about our emotional journey may help you understand what they are feeling and experiencing.

We are just one family, but I think we are a fair representation of the many suicide loss survivor families in the world today. Suicide *loss* survivors are the loved ones (families, friends, and others who care) left behind after a suicide. Suicide *attempt* survivors are those people who attempted suicide and survived. Now if God forbid, you are contemplating taking your life, then please use this opportunity to see all that your friends and family might go through if they lose you. Hopefully, this encourages you to *stay* and reach out to get the help you need.

The grieving process is complicated and hard work, but it is not a villain or an enemy. It is a necessary way we cleanse and work through our sorrow so we can engage in life again. Tom, Kelli, and I started the grieving process from the moment we heard Nick had jumped. The first few days after you experience a tragedy of this magnitude, you seem to go into a type of shock as your body protects you from a total shutdown or heart attack. You may not realize you are in shock, but others probably see signs of it in you, like being spacey and in a daze. You can think some pretty "out there" thoughts, do some strange things, and feel like you are out of control, even losing your mind.

One instance still stands out for me. I was home alone in Tom's office rocking back and forth on my knees in front of a large framed collage of Nick's pictures hanging on the wall. I found myself repeating over and over like I was in a trance, "You killed yourself, and you're *not* coming back, you killed yourself, and you're *never* coming back." I was trying to make the magnitude and finality of Nick's suicide sink in because I was having a hard time mentally processing what had just happened. It all seemed so surreal. If anyone had looked through the window, they would have thought I had lost my sanity for sure.

We cried all the time, partly as some subconscious release of visceral pain that was almost too intense for our bodies to handle. Then at some point, we became numb. It was like we had reached a plateau, or saturation point, making it impossible to feel any more emotional pain. Our bodies or minds—maybe both— wouldn't let us. We were still feeling pain, but it was all at one level. It wasn't stress: the two don't even compare. The pain was so intense, we felt like we could almost lose our minds from it all. But somehow, we went on.

When people came to our door to pay their respects, we put on brave faces but were hurting badly. Tom and Kelli appreciated that people were supporting us by dropping off food and checking to see if we were okay, but sometimes they needed to

excuse themselves and go upstairs to be alone and mourn. I, however, was healing more by reaching outward and talking about it
with our visitors. Tom, Kelli, and I realized we each were grieving
differently and knew we had to respect and honor what each
needed to feel better. When I look back, I am so grateful we were
able to do this and be kind to one another throughout the whole
grieving process because I know some families have difficulties
doing so. Each one of us was going through hell, and the last thing
we needed was to be at each other's throats. That extra stress
would have significantly hindered our healing.

If you are grieving with your family or friends, please try to
give each other space and time to mourn in your own ways. Be
patient and kind to one another and cut each other a lot of slack
because what you are going through is extraordinarily demanding
on everyone involved. Mutual respect is not only helpful but necessary for healing.

Tom, Kelli, and I were mourning in our own ways, but we all
agreed on how grueling it must have been for people to muster up
the courage to ring our doorbell. Everyone probably thought the
same thing, "What in the heck can I say to those poor people?" It
is hard enough to find the words when someone dies, but when it
is suicide—and of a young person . . . well, it doesn't get much
tougher than that. I imagine many people struggled to say the
right thing, and some even worried they would put their foot in
their mouth. I would be thinking the same if I were them, but
there was not much anyone could say that would be wrong.

Being told things like, "Nick is in a better place now," never
bothered me because I agree; he's in a better place. I, too, believe
heaven's our home and is much better than here. Even if someone had said something a little off, I would have understood
because most people mean well but sometimes get nervous. If
you have difficulties finding the right words to share with

someone after they have lost a loved one, don't worry too much about saying the wrong thing. Just let them know you care and are always there for them if they ever want to talk. Your good intentions will shine through, no matter what words you choose. If they are super-sensitive to your word choice, then try to be understanding. They will come around.

THOSE DIFFICULT FEW VISITORS

People can say awkward things, which mourners should do their best to overlook, but there are also rare times when people in grief need to protect themselves from outsiders who are not paying their respects so much as being either nosy or overly insensitive, causing more pain.

A husband and wife came to see us whom we had not seen or heard from for almost ten years. Nick had just died two days earlier, and it was the second night after my return from Minneapolis. By the end of the evening, Tom and I were exhausted from talking with all our lovely friends and neighbors who stopped by to show their support. Everyone left at a reasonable hour, understanding we needed our rest—but this couple stayed behind. Keeping us up wasn't the worst part, though. Around midnight, as the four of us sat around the kitchen table visiting, the wife's eyes suddenly got big and started to roll back in her head. She got this glazed look on her face as she began to talk in a low, monotone voice. Seeing that Tom and I were utterly dumbfounded, the husband explained that she had the ability to "channel" Nick.

We found ourselves in the middle of a séance. I'm trying to be kind here and shell out a tremendous amount of benefit of a doubt when I say that, even if by some chance she could connect with Nick at our kitchen table, now was not the time. For the love of

God, our child had just died. To say we wanted to ask them to leave is a magnificent understatement, but we were just too vulnerable and broken. Around 4 a.m., they laughed and said they should go because they had probably overstayed their welcome.

Over the next five weeks the woman called daily to tell me Nick was visiting her family. She chuckled as she conveyed how much Nick loved sitting in her kitchen and talking with her while she cooked and regularly hung out with her teenage daughter. Although her calls caused me much pain, I tried to be nice and didn't say much. I let her talk. Then one day she said something that caused the hair on the back of my neck to stand up—that she was keeping Nick safe inside her stomach. I mean, how do you respond to something like that? I was silent. She must have sensed I'd had enough because that was her last call, and we never heard from that couple again.

Why is it that tragedies seem to bring out the best and worst in people? Which, by the way, is one more Law of the Universe. So as a recap, telling people their loved one is now in a better place or saying practically anything else—acceptable. Assuring them you are keeping their loved one safe inside your stomach—not so much.

WOULD-HAVES, COULD-HAVES, AND SHOULD-HAVES

We could not shut our minds off day or night reliving the last moments with Nick and asking ourselves what signs we missed and what more we could have done. My final conversations with him played and replayed in my head. In fact, all three of us were doing that. We were mentally trying to rewrite what happened because we felt guilty for things we did or failed to do. The would-haves, could-haves, and should-haves kept looping in our heads, and each time they circled, they took a little piece of us.

Day and night, I beat myself up over letting Nick go to class, even after seeing how upset he was those last moments. I kept asking myself why I didn't just grab him, take him home to a doctor, or take him to a hospital in Minnesota. If Nick's issue had been physical instead of mental, I would have known exactly what to do. With a 102-degree fever, realizing the need to get help at the medical clinic on campus would have been a no-brainer, but when it came to a mental health issue, I, like so many people, was at a loss. I knew something was wrong with Nick but never thought he was suicidal.

Just eight days earlier, he had mentioned for the first time he was depressed, but what I saw in Jamba Juice was more than depression. I wasn't exactly sure what it was, but it seemed like a disconnect of some kind. Also, he showed a hint of paranoia that last weekend, but I didn't even know that for sure. I thought he could stay at school the final two weeks before the summer break, especially since I was there with him and figured he was well enough to make it through his last classes and finals. The plan was to fly home together and get him help immediately afterward. Because I did not think he was suicidal and was not aware people had jumped off those bridges near the University of Minnesota, I had no idea I was risking Nick's life by letting him leave my sight that final day.

And what parent yanks their kid out of college right before finals? In hindsight, I wish it were me. My kids always told me I was an overprotective mother with a tendency to overreact. Well, I picked a fine time to stop doing that. I never had the chance to figure out what was going on with Nick because he never came home from class that day. Learn from what happened to us: when you see your loved ones hurting in ways that are more than being a little down, do not think they can power through it for any length of time, not even for two weeks, and regardless of whether they are about to do something as important as taking finals. Err on the side of caution.

Kelli was going through her own hell. She felt guilty for not texting and emailing Nick the last few weeks as often as she usually did. Like the rest of us, she had no idea he was suffering so much and was suicidal. I will tell you more about her grief process in chapter 10.

Tom, like the rest of us, felt terrible for not realizing Nick was in pain and was beating himself up over letting Nick go to a college seven hours from home. He had taken Nick on thirteen college visits over the eighteen months before freshman year and spent a lot of time talking with Nick during those visits. Tom, like the two psychologists who saw Nick in high school, felt he was ready and able to go away to school. Now he believed he had failed to protect his child from harm.

We all felt like we had failed Nick. How could we miss that he was in so much pain, a pain so intense the only option he could see to free himself was to end his life? We were a close-knit family and loved each other very much, so how did this happen? Hindsight is painful because things you missed jump out screaming at you, options suddenly become apparent, and ways you could have handled matters differently become obvious. But that is not how people live their lives. We do not have a crystal ball, and we are imperfect beings. Our interactions with one another are dependent on our human limitations and what others are willing to show us. I had to keep reminding myself of this to heal. We all had to—and still do.

We did not sleep more than a few hours a night for the first month. We tossed and turned in anguish, withering in grief. When we did doze off, waking up was painful because, during that first second, we had to "re-remember" what happened to Nick. But for a fraction of that first second, it all seemed like just a terrible nightmare. We also didn't feel much like eating. Heavy food did not go down well because our stomachs were queasy from grief, and we were dehydrated from crying so much. We lived on fresh fruit and soup because they were both light and hydrating.

A friend who lost her son in Afghanistan told me to stay away from music for a while because it would evoke emotions and memories that would make me feel even worse. Oh, was she right. I regretted not taking her advice. The Carrie Underwood song "Till I See You Again" had just hit the charts, and radio stations were playing it over and over. To this day, every time I hear it, my heart feels like it is shattering. The lyrics, about how someone turned around and a loved one slipped away, hit home a little too hard. I eventually started listening exclusively to upbeat Christian music, which seemed to help me heal.

Long ago I read somewhere that when you love with all you have, you grieve with all you are. So, when you look at how much you are grieving, let it serve as a reminder of the love you shared. Our grieving continued well past these first days and changed with time, which I will explain later, but for now, it is essential to tell Nick's story chronologically, just how it unfolded for us.

Chapter 6

The Memorial Service

Nick's body was lost for weeks, making it impossible to have a funeral right away. After a long month of waiting to see if his body would surface, we decided to go ahead and have a memorial mass because, like the Minneapolis detective warned, his body might never be found. Tom and I waited long enough for the high school and college students to finish finals so they could attend Nick's memorial if they wished. We scheduled it for the Saturday of Memorial Day weekend.

Right after Nick died, one of my friends warned me that the Catholic Church would probably not allow us to have a Christian mass of burial because Nick killed himself. That turned out to be wrong. It was true years ago, but not now. The 1997 *Catechism of the Catholic Church* states, "Grave psychological disturbances, anguish, or grave fear of hardship, suffering, or torture can diminish the responsibility of one committing suicide" (550, #2282).[1] It seems to me that almost every case of suicide involves grave psychological disturbances, anguish, or grave fear of hardship, suffering, or torture. I learned it is no longer forbidden by canon law to hold funeral rites for people who take their own lives.[2] In other words, if your loved one dies by suicide, and you are a Catholic, do not let anyone convince you that your family cannot have a funeral mass in a Catholic church or burial in a Catholic cemetery.

I have to digress here and share that from the time Nick passed, I've had many people tell me they pray for Nick every day, which is incredibly kind. However, a few have said it in a way that leads me to believe they think my son is burning in hell, and they are praying to help save his soul. Those beliefs used to bother me, especially knowing how loving Nick was, but now they don't as much. If you have lost someone to suicide and also have experienced this, try to let it roll off your back. People sometimes are hardwired to judge, especially when it comes to unfamiliar territory, like mental illness. And if they are not judging but merely following outdated religious dogma, or what they think is dogma, understand that in their minds, they mean well. They are trying to do what they feel is best for your loved one. Just let it go.

During Nick's junior and senior years, he was an altar server for Mass at a Catholic monastery of Benedictine monks with a few other boys from his high school. He became friends with many of the monks who resided there. Five of them, who were priests, came over to our parish and celebrated Nick's memorial mass with our pastor. The abbot of the monastery gave a comforting and inspirational homily (lecture). It was a beautiful, healing sight to see so many Catholic priests on the altar, especially for those people attending who were not aware of the Church's position on suicide. They were all compassionate and loving toward Nick and our family and were instrumental in our healing.

Many of the kids from Nick's high school participated in the memorial as ushers, altar servers, and choir members. One of Kelli's high school classmates played bagpipes as people walked into church, testing everyone's ability to hold back tears. All these incredibly kind people gave up their Memorial Day cookouts and cheerful family get-togethers to support us. The entire church was filled with our family, friends, coworkers, neighbors, teachers, students, and more. Tom, Kelli, and I were overwhelmed by the turnout and believed Nick would have been too. In fact, he would have been amazed and, knowing him, humbled that so many people cared about him. Everywhere we looked, there were people we knew from all parts of our lives—past and present. The outpouring of love and support held the three of us up.

Many high schoolers and college students sang in the choir, including Jennie, a beautiful young girl with a tremendous spirit who was a year younger than Nick. Sadly, Jennie was fatally struck by lightning less than two weeks later while sitting in a park writing in her journal. I will never forget that one of Jennie's last acts of kindness in this world was to give up her holiday weekend to sing at Nick's mass.

Often when I visit Nick's gravesite, I walk over to Jennie's located about a hundred yards away and say a few prayers. Someone told me that she was broken up after hearing Nick died. I remember her coming up to me at the end of Nick's memorial mass with tears in her eyes to tell me how much she liked Nick and was going to miss him. The sweetness that emanated from Jennie reminded me of my son. A few weeks later when I learned of her passing, I bowed my head and asked Nick to go find his friend on the other side and be with her. I have no doubts that the two of them are happy and looking out for the rest of us.

A few of Nick's high school friends who served with him at the monastery volunteered to be altar servers for his mass. Our entire church was filled. Many high school students, as well as kids from Nick's graduating class who came home from college, attended the memorial. Except for one or two, every teacher Nick ever had from kindergarten on up was there. I spoke with Nick's second-grade teacher afterward and expressed how grateful and surprised I was that so many of them came to pay their respects.

I will never forget her response. She said students come and go, but now and then teachers get a student they will always remember because he or she was so special. She told me Nick was that student for many of them. Her words meant so very much to me—and still do.

Directly following Mass, something very special happened. We had asked permission from the clergy to allow people to come up to the podium (ambo) and say a few words once the mass ended. We thought this might be healing for the kids. Following our dear friend Rudy's heartfelt eulogy, one by one, the teenagers spoke about how Nick had affected their lives. They each shared their gratitude for his life while testifying to his character. These testimonies went on for forty-five minutes straight until a clergy member finally asked the kids to wrap it up due to time constraints.

My gosh, I wanted to send Nick off with a mass that would show him how much he was appreciated and loved in this life because I knew he could not fully feel it while he was here, but this memorial went well beyond what I could have ever imagined. If only Nick had realized how many people cared for him, maybe he would still be here.

I cannot adequately put into words how healing this memorial was for us and how much Tom, Kelli, and I appreciated it. That evening was the first time since Nick passed that Tom and I slept through the entire night. It was a turning point in my family's healing.

I wish every person who feels sad and lonely could see all the people who had attended Nick's memorial and listen to what the kids had to say about their friend so eloquently and from their hearts. I'm not sharing all of this to say, "Hey, look how many people liked my kid," but rather to point out that we are all loved *way* more than we realize in this life. Remember, Nick never thought he had many friends. He was sad and lonely, and he had no idea people cared so deeply. I think we *all* have more people in our lives who care for us than we realize. Every one of us positively affects a significantly larger number than we ever could imagine. We need to remind ourselves of these things whenever we feel down and all alone.

The people who showed up for Nick represent all the people in every one of our lives, even when our minds may not let us believe or feel they are out there caring for us. If you are reading this and think no one gives a damn about you, and your life doesn't matter, be open to the very real possibility that you may be hurting so much you cannot feel the affection of others—or you perceive that affection differently. Perhaps you are focusing on the wrong people when trying to find friends and companions. Maybe you are trying to be a member of a group that might not be the best fit for you.

Be careful not to shut out those people in the periphery of your life who genuinely care about you. I think Nick did that sometimes. He was so worried about fitting into a particular group that he missed people in another who wanted to be his friend. Maybe Nick did have Asperger's, and it kept him from feeling some of the emotions of others. Perhaps he was depressed and could not look beyond his sadness. I don't know and never will. But the real message here is that Nick had more people in his life who cared about him than he ever realized, and you most likely do too.

Chapter 7

Body Is Found, and Videos Appear

BODY IDENTIFIED, AND ASHES COME HOME

A few days after the memorial mass, a fisherman found Nick's body many miles from where he jumped. I never learned the nitty-gritty details about the discovery and never want to either. His body had been in the water for almost five weeks, so we had no choice but to cremate his remains in Minnesota.

The identification process did not go smoothly. Remember just a week earlier, the coroner told us he had Nick's body, but he was mistaken. At that time, I asked him if he was sure it was Nick's because I saw a newspaper article about the Wisconsin boy, who jumped into the Mississippi one week later, and noticed how similar they looked. With my prompting, he double-checked the identification by using the Wisconsin boy's dental records and discovered his error.

This time, the coroner was careful not to cause us any more pain. He waited a day to call so he could make the identification using the dental records we sent after the first mishap. The body was Nick's.

All the calls with the coroner's office about sending the dental records of Nick, finding the body of Nick, the body not being

Nick, still looking for Nick, and finally finding Nick were all coming in on our home phone while poor Kelli was trying to concentrate on studying for her high school final exams. Can you
imagine? Knowing how difficult this was on Tom and me, having
had years to build coping skills, we could not begin to understand
how Kelli was handling all this. She was just seventeen, an age
when her focus should have been on things like school, friends,
and junior prom. She was being exposed to way too much, but
there was nowhere for her to escape.

No mother or father should have to talk to a coroner about
their child—ever. Later in the day as I was returning one of the
many coroner calls, a female examiner answered the phone. She
must have been newly assigned to the case. I don't know why, but
I had to tell her who she had in front of her on the table—that not
only was he my sweet boy, but he was the most loving, kind, and
gentle person I had ever met. It was important to me that she
knew it. I give this woman a lot of credit because she did not rush
me off the phone or act too clinical. Instead, she patiently listened
as I rambled on, even as I became aware I was sounding slightly
pathetic.

A few days later our friend Rudy drove Tom to Minneapolis
to get Nick's ashes so Tom wouldn't have to make the gut-wrenching, thirteen-hour trip there and back alone. I stayed home with
Kelli. The whole time Tom was gone I kept thinking about how
Nick left for his freshman year in August, like most kids, with big
dreams, high hopes, and a car filled to the brim with teenage
possessions and now was coming home in an urn wrapped in the
arms of his grieving father.

When I heard the garage door open, my heart sank. I was
sitting on the couch. Tom walked through the door. As he walked
toward me, I could see his eyes were red from crying. He gently

placed Nick's urn into my arms, and at that moment, I knew for sure my heart was broken . . . no, *I* was broken. Visions of me holding Nick as a baby flashed in my head. Then, I thought of Michelangelo's *Pietà*, the famous sculpture of Mary holding the body of Jesus in her arms after His death. My grief could never compare, but now, I had a better understanding.

VIDEOS

As if mourning Nick's suicide wasn't grueling enough, two horrible videos about his death surfaced online, and we had to figure out how to remove them from the internet. A few weeks after Nick passed, Tom's sister called to tell us there was a video on YouTube that we needed to get removed, immediately. It featured a University of Minnesota student Nick knew and was entitled, "The Gospel via Nick Pacha." The video, taken during a class, showed a young man, whom I will call Rick, standing in front of a classroom of students. He was wearing a gray T-shirt and dark pink ball cap that was turned backward.

Interestingly, Rick was one of the guys who strung Nick along on the apartment lease and, therefore, was not a friend to Nick. But on this day, he told the class that while all of them "were having fun and partying" last weekend, their "good friend" jumped off a bridge and killed himself. Then Rick began an over-the-top rant, saying things like:

> *I have been praying for every one of you because the last thing I want to see is for someone to perish and go to hell. Heaven is not for good people, but for people who have admitted they are not good enough; this is why we need Jesus. We all deserve hell.*

He ended his speech with some advice for the female students in the room:

> *Girls, you think your boyfriends are going to free you?*
> *They can't. But Jesus can, and he will. Boyfriends are*
> *great, but they're not Jesus. For a lot of you, your*
> *boyfriends are Jesus, and* Cosmo *[Cosmopolitan] is*
> *your Bible. It's time for that to stop.*

Rick clearly enjoyed hearing himself speak, and I'm guessing he didn't date much after that day. I support his right to free speech, but not his use of my deceased son's name or his exploitation of Nick's death for dramatic effect. And why post something so inflammatory on YouTube and entitle it in a way that sounds like it was Nick's personal view? It really upset me that this guy was trying to make the world believe Nick shared his crazy beliefs when nothing could have been further from the truth. Nick had strong faith that was loving, not radical, and always had the utmost respect for women. Kelli and I can attest to that. Nick would have even cringed at using a word like "via."

Tom reached out to the Minneapolis detective who was working on Nick's case, the same guy who came to my hotel room the day Nick passed, and sent him a link to the video. The detective was equally disgusted by this guy's insensitivity and said he would try to get him to take it down. In the meantime, we contacted YouTube to help us, and I found Rick on Facebook, so I posted that I would take legal action against him if he didn't immediately remove the video.

Later that afternoon, the detective called to tell us he had strongly encouraged Rick to do the right thing but didn't know if he would remove it because he appeared to be a little unstable. Ultimately, I'm not sure how the video came down—if Rick voluntarily deleted it, or if the people at YouTube removed it. By the end of the evening, only the title remained online, which was searchable for quite some time. Eventually, it also disappeared.

A second video created by some other young males surfaced a few weeks later. One of our neighbors brought it to our attention, and this one was even more vile because it made fun of Nick's death. She found the video online before she left for vacation but was afraid to tell us because we had gone through so much already. When we told her about the first video, she informed us about the second.

The video showed three college-age boys all in swimming trunks. Two of them were standing on a low bridge that hung over a small river. The third guy, filming the event from the nearby riverbank, announced, "Nick Pacha jumping from a bridge." The two boys jumped from the bridge into the water and swam to their friend. As they got out of the water, they laughed and continued laughing, then all got into a car and drove away. How's that for evil?

My neighbor searched to see if the video was still online when she returned from her vacation, but it was gone. Tom and I spent the next few days searching on the internet but could not find any traces of it. Maybe these boys, whom we did not know, got wind of the detective talking to Rick about his video, got scared, and took theirs down. Or perhaps they saw my post on Rick's Facebook threatening legal action. I don't know what happened, but I'm relieved it came down.

From that point forward, some of our friends and family volunteered to protect us by doing daily searches online looking for any additional postings and videos about Nick. Like I said before, tragedy brings out the best and worst in people. Sadly, even in death, Nick was bullied.

Chapter 8

Bullying and Social Difficulties

❋ **Empathy:** the action of understanding, being aware of, being sensitive to, and vicariously experiencing the feelings, thoughts, and experience of another of either the past or present without having the feelings, thoughts, and experience fully communicated in an objectively explicit manner

❋ **Compassion:** sympathetic consciousness of others' distress together with a desire to alleviate it

❋ **Inclusion:** the act of including: the state of being included

—*Merriam-Webster Dictionary*

Throughout Nick's life, people disappointed and hurt him. In grade school, a few kids threatened to beat him up, but I don't think anyone laid a hand on him. If any kids did, Nick never told us about it. He was, however, verbally bullied. This caused him a great amount of emotional pain, but so did not fitting in well with his peers, being excluded from friendship groups and activities, not receiving responses to his calls and texts, and hearing unkind comments that did not rise to the level of bullying. All of these things happened so frequently, and for so long, there was a cumulative effect on him. By the time Nick reached his late teens, each time someone treated him rudely or like he was invisible, he could no longer see that behavior as *one* unkind action or *one* painful event, but instead as that individual rejecting him entirely as a *person*. He was not overly sensitive when he was little, but the unkindness directed at him over the years stacked on top of his loneliness, causing his pain to go so deep it became a mortal wound. Rejection upon rejection piled up and eventually buried his hope for ever having a happy future.

People may think they are dissing someone for one brief moment or are giving only one good insult, but they have no idea how much that person may have taken over the years. Likewise, kids who do not respond to someone's text or phone call may not think twice about it, but the individual they are too busy to answer, or don't want to make time for, may have been ignored by countless other people in the past. That one action, or inaction, could be magnified by a thousand in the recipient's mind, making it impossible for him or her not to take personally. Instead, it sticks and burrows in, causing deep pain.

Conversely, one compliment instead of an insult or diss—one kind text, phone call, or even a smile—can make a huge difference in a lonely person's life. It can comfort and offer hope to someone who is hurting.

Seeing how hurt Nick became when people treated him poorly, and how much he struggled with his mental health, has given me more compassion toward others who may be going through difficult times. Whenever people cut me off in traffic or are rude to me, I try to remember that I don't know what they are going through. They may be mentally ill, or perhaps they just got fired from a job. Maybe they just got diagnosed with cancer or are drowning in debt. Nick's struggles opened my eyes as to how important it is to show *all* people compassion and kindness. The happiness of others may depend on it, and it can even save lives.

Dealing with bullying was hard enough for Nick, but he was also challenged with other social difficulties, such as being confused about his sexual orientation. Many times, these issues overlapped. Allow me to share chronologically how they all affected Nick throughout his school years.

GRADE SCHOOL

Nick had a third-grade bully who had been mean to him since the first grade and occasionally said he wanted to fight Nick. Whenever this kid got picked up by his dad from school, you could hear the father's yelling from the car window. I had a feeling this was a peek into this boy's family life, and he was bullying Nick as a way to vent his built-up frustrations from his father's constant ridicule. I felt bad for this kid, but he was still my son's bully. After school one day, I walked up to him as he stood alone waiting for his dad and told him he better leave Nick alone, or I would go to his house and let his parents know about his bullying. I can't remember what else I said to him, but it worked because from that point forward, he stopped picking on Nick. I got lucky. My intervention worked only because the boys were young, but it easily could have backfired, causing Nick even more grief. The right thing to do was to take my complaint to the school administrators.

MIDDLE SCHOOL

I know of four boys in middle school who made Nick's life miserable, but Kelli told me there were more. They would call him names, make fun of him in front of other kids, and laugh at him. Nick would come into the car after school and tell Kelli and me whenever he had a bad day, and there were many. This bullying happened in the early 2000s when it was not on everyone's radar as much as it is now. Partly this was because it was not as prevalent then, and when it did occur, parents were less likely to report it to the school administration, especially when the bullying was not physical.

There was one bully I did not learn about until many years later. When Nick was in middle school, we signed him up for Boy Scouts. Tom and I were thrilled to get him in with a nice group of boys who seemed friendly and supportive, so you can imagine our shock when Nick begged us to quit Scouts a few months later. We kept asking him why he wanted to drop out when he finally got involved with such kind kids. Quitting made no sense to us because we knew how much Nick wanted that type of camaraderie. Nevertheless, he was insistent he didn't like Scouting, so we finally let him quit.

Years later, Nick finally told us the real reason he dropped out. He said one of the boys in his troop had been bullying him since grade school. When Nick was about to graduate high school and move on to college, the boy finally came to him and apologized for making his life miserable over the past eleven years. Eleven years! Nick came home from high school that day and told us about all of it, and that this boy was the reason he quit Scouts so many years earlier. Can you imagine being bullied by the same person for that many years?

Tom and I felt sick when we found out. My gosh, we unknowingly made him go to Boy Scouts with his biggest bully. If Nick had told us his reason for wanting to quit back then, he could have transferred to another troop and been happy. And maybe, just maybe, he would have made good friends. We'll never know. I imagine after this kid heard Nick was bullied in college and died by suicide, he must have been relieved he apologized to Nick for bullying him all those years. Nick told me that when this kid finally apologized at the end of high school, he shook the boy's hand in forgiveness.

Lunchtime

Nick was sad he didn't have friends to sit with at lunch. He dreaded lunchtime every single day, like most kids who do not have many friends. For the socially challenged, the lunch hour seems about ten hours long, and the whole time they feel like they have a spotlight on their heads. Unfortunately, even in high school, lunchtime did not get much better for Nick. During his middle school years, he often ate his sandwich in the bathroom, and in a guidance counselor's office when he was in high school.

I wish *all* schools would implement programs to help kids who struggle to find table companions, such as the following (some are my ideas and others I have heard about):

Volunteer Role Models

Identify those kids who need a tablemate. Student council members, Boy Scouts, Girl Scouts, sports team leaders, and any other volunteers discreetly identify kids who are sitting alone and sit with them, modeling kindness and inclusion for the rest of the student body.

Round Tables

Equip lunchrooms with more round tables. Rounds are more conducive than long tables for group conversation and allow kids to feel surrounded by their peers. Even though round tables have fewer seats and take up more space, it's helpful to include a few of them in the lunchroom because they are an excellent option for kids who feel more isolated at long tables.

Buddy System

Pair kids up with a buddy. Kids needing a tablemate give their names confidentially to a teacher who discreetly matches them up to sit together for the day. Name submissions and seating assignments can be done online the day prior and matched confidentially.

Rotating Seating

Designate one or two tables in a lunchroom for rotated seating. Kids sign up online or in person with a teacher for a seat at one of those tables that have seating designated by a number. After all sign-ups are submitted, the kids are randomly assigned a number, leaving no empty seats. Table assignments can be made daily, weekly, or as needed.

Big Sister–Little Sister/Big Brother–Little Brother

Match kids up with a designated "sibling." Younger kids interested in the program sign up to be paired with older kids whose participation is also voluntary. At least one designated day a week, kids eat lunch together with their assigned big brother or sister.

Tables by Topics

Designate tables by topics of interest. Kids eat lunch at a few tables designated by special interests, such as book club readers, game players (computer, chess, checkers, etc.), or various hobbies. Partition and label tables accordingly. This program helps those having difficulties making everyday conversation by allowing them to discuss their shared interest while eating lunch.

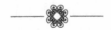

The real key is to teach kids about empathy, compassion, and inclusion from preschool through the various grade levels, so they develop a strong social conscience. The hope is that they will be more willing to seek out peers who are sitting alone and invite them to join their lunch tables and friend groups. I will talk more about this in chapter 18.

Gym Class

Another part of the school day that every kid with social challenges dreads is physical education or gym class. We all know that not every kid is good at sports. For those students who are athletically inept, socially awkward, or both, the nightmare begins when teams are picked. Teams are chosen today just as they were years ago: two team captains look the class over and select the most athletic kids first, then the "coolest" kids second. Often the athletic kids *are* considered the cool kids, as they were generations ago. After the team captain chooses the first kids, the newly selected scream out the names of who they think the captain should choose next. As more kids are picked, the number of kids yelling gets larger and larger, and they shout their opinions louder and louder. Toward the end of the selection process, there's pretty much a mob consensus about which kids should be left until last. I remember from my school days kids yelling things like, "Don't pick Timmy. He sucks!"

I know it has always been done this way, but the whole process is demeaning and demoralizing. Think about it—these kids probably just sat alone at lunch, and now they are picked dead last with all their peers yelling to choose any other kids besides them. And this happens to them five days out of seven, during each week of the school year. Day in and day out, fitting in and finding friends wears on their mental health. Those who think this sounds a little over the top, ask yourself—where in the order were you picked?

We have to try a better system. Look at what's happening in our world today. More and more, young people are killing themselves—even kids in grade school. A lack of meaningful socialization, together with repetitive exclusion, leads to isolation and lowered self-confidence. As a society, we cannot stick to what we have always done because it's just not working anymore. We must take a closer look at the school day and change things. To choose teams, can't the kids draw numbers out of a hat or something? What if the teacher uses a computer application to create teams? The teacher privately enters the skill level for each student into a program that creates teams evenly matched based on the skill level of the team as a whole. There has to be an application for something like that in existence—if not, someone please create one.

Calls, Texts, and No Responses

When Nick was in middle school, kids were starting to get cell phones. At first, he was thrilled to get one, but that excitement quickly wore off when he began to text and call kids but received very few responses. This happened over and over again. If Nick didn't hear back from someone, he would agonize about whether he should text or call again. He wanted to make sure his classmate got the message but didn't want to appear needy. Nick came to realize that kids usually received his communications but were either too busy to respond or didn't bother answering, so his phone became one more way to get rejected. I cannot tell you how many times I walked by his room and saw him looking down at his phone with a hurt look on his face. It always broke my heart.

There were three boys Nick considered friends whom he would text and call quite often. One of the boys was a better friend to Nick than the other two, but that is not saying a great deal because none of them really wanted to hang out with him very much. They were going through some of their own issues and were not considerate about responding whenever Nick reached out to them. None of them had many friends. Tom, Kelli, and I kept telling Nick not to feel bad whenever he didn't hear from them and just move on, but for some reason, Nick felt some loyalty to these three and continued to reach out to them throughout middle school and high school.

Finally, an Invite

One day Nick came home from middle school all excited because a boy asked him to come over after school to hang out. For most kids, this occurred all the time and was no big deal, but it never happened for Nick. During the entire car ride there, Nick told me how excited he was to finally have a friend to hang with outside of school. I rang the doorbell to introduce myself to his parents, and the father answered. The mother didn't appear to be around, but the dad assured me he would be home the whole time Nick was there. I drove away so happy for Nick and looked forward to him telling me all about his new friend when I picked him up later. Maybe Nick was finally getting that best friend he always wanted.

Less than an hour after being dropped off, Nick called saying he wanted to get picked up right away. He sounded either scared or panicked; I wasn't sure which. When I asked what happened, he said he would tell me later but to hurry. We lived about five minutes from the boy's house, and I pulled in their driveway in two. My car had not even come to a complete stop when Nick flew out the front door and into the car. His eyes were big, leaving no doubt that he was panicked. Nick shot me down with one word when I tried to ask about it: "Drive!"

As we pulled away, he burst into tears and began to tell me how he and the boy were hanging out in his room when suddenly the kid got up, left the room, and came back wearing a pair of gym shorts. He told Nick he wanted to wrestle and before Nick knew it, he was thrown facedown onto the floor with the kid on top of him rubbing himself against Nick's back and reaching under to grab Nick's private parts. He shoved the kid off and shouted, "What the hell are you doing?" Nick said that's when he grabbed his phone and called me. Nick ran out of the kid's room and stood waiting for me at the front door. I asked where the father was this whole time, but Nick didn't know. He thought he was somewhere inside the house.

I was furious. I wanted to go yell at the father and was tempted to do far worse to the kid, but Nick pleaded with me to keep driving. He didn't want to go back there, and after thinking about it for a moment, I agreed that would have only traumatized Nick more.

Once home, I had to calm myself down a little before I called, but that effort went to hell when the father told me his son claimed that Nick pulled up bad websites on the computer in his room. Really? Your kid just assaulted my son, and you're going to accuse mine of exposing yours to porn under your roof, under your watch, and on your son's personal computer? I was insistent that Nick would never do that. I kept repeating how traumatized Nick was when he ran out of his house, which told me Nick was telling the truth about everything. I asked the father, "If my son was there enjoying himself looking at porn, why would he leave so soon and fly out the door in a sheer panic?" The conversation went nowhere from there because it was his son's word against Nick's.

After hanging up, I sat down with Nick and told him about our conversation. Nick was upset that the boy lied and said they never went on his computer the entire time he was there. He swore he was telling the truth, and I believed him. It all made sense with what I witnessed when I pulled into that driveway. Later that evening, Tom and I asked Nick if he wanted to talk to a counselor about what happened, but Nick said he was all right and just wanted to forget it ever happened.

A few days later, the father called to apologize and assure me Nick was being truthful with me. The dad did some extensive search through his son's computer history and saw for himself that the computer had never been turned on the entire time Nick was in his home. He found gay porn all over the computer that his son had been watching for quite some time, but not when Nick was there. The father, defeated and embarrassed, apologized over and over to me. I was angry that his son was able to do that to Nick when he should have been overseeing the boys, but I appreciated that he at least had the decency to let me know Nick was telling the truth.

Tom and I didn't want this boy to traumatize any other kids, so we talked about the possibility of telling the middle school administrators what happened. The incident, however, didn't happen on school property, so it was not a school matter. Also, Nick was afraid that if we brought it to the school's attention, all the kids would find out. If we took it to the police, the kid would just say he was "wrestling" with Nick, which was not a crime. We had no choice but to let it go. At least the kid's father knew what happened. The boy was a minor, and it was up to the father to get him professional help. It was so sad—here Nick finally got invited to some boy's home to hang out, and that happened.

HIGH SCHOOL

Nick was excited to start high school because he saw it as a new opportunity to make friends. He went to an excellent private, college preparatory Catholic high school. The school was small, and all the kids eventually got to know one another. If a kid wasn't your friend, he or she was at least an acquaintance.

The first few months of freshman year, Nick was happy because some of the kids thought he looked like the singer Brendon Urie from *Panic! At the Disco*. What teenager wouldn't like that attention? Nick's teachers often complimented me about Nick and told me he had a reputation among the staff as being a good and honest kid. He was off to a good start, but over time, I noticed he started having difficulties fitting in with some of the kids, as he did in earlier school years, but could not understand why.

Lunchtime

Lunchtime was still difficult for Nick in high school. He dreaded that hour every single day and ate many lunches in a counselor's office with a few other kids who struggled socially. I am so grateful to this thoughtful woman counselor for being so kind to Nick, and having the insight to know some kids need a place to escape, a type of safe zone, at lunchtime.

Band

Both of my kids were in band since fourth grade: Nick played the trumpet and Kelli played the saxophone. When Nick was having a difficult time making friends in middle school, I kept telling him his social life would improve once he was in the high school band program. That is where I made most of my friends in high school. We used to go out after practice and have a lot of fun. I wanted Nick to have that same experience, so I talked up the band program at his high school and gave him high hopes for making friends there.

I never would have guessed that any band kid would be mean to Nick, but a few of them made his time in that organization one of the worst experiences of his short life. It's a shame because typically music students look out for one another. Even in Nick's band, most of the kids were caring and fun-loving, except for the few who treated my son with such disregard for his feelings—or for him as a human being.

One day during marching band practice, Nick and another boy quipped back and forth on the football field. One thing led to another, and the kid suddenly turned to Nick and said, "Why don't you go kill yourself?" Wow! Can someone please tell me when that's ever okay to say? That remark hurt Nick so much it made him break down and cry when he told me about it later that evening.

You know, I have thought about that young man many times after Nick's death. He was not a bad kid by any means. He's now in a service-oriented career, which makes me think he must be a caring young man. But as a young teenager, he didn't realize how repugnant and cruel his words were to Nick. I hope, for his sake, he doesn't remember telling Nick to go kill himself; but if he does, I pray he has forgiven himself, especially after hearing Nick had mental health issues and died by suicide. If Nick had already started thinking about taking his life back then, I wonder what he must have felt when someone told him to go do it.

Another time, the high school band was playing for a pep rally before one of the school's basketball games. Nick was either walking from the gym to the band room or vice versa, and two guys with a girl from the band followed closely behind him. One of the boys made fun of the way Nick walked, and the girl burst out laughing. Nick overheard them and was in so much pain he ducked into a nearby bathroom and sat alone on the floor crying against a stall until he could calm himself and return to the gymnasium where the rest of the band was having a good time playing for the rally. Being laughed at hurt, like it always did, but this time it was even more crushing because Nick had known that girl for many years and considered her to be someone he could trust. He never expected that type of treatment from her.

Over the years, this girl matured into a fabulous young woman, who I know would feel terrible if she learned she hurt a "friend" so profoundly. Some people don't realize how their words, actions, and even inactions can have such a devastating impact on others. This treatment toward Nick was all awful, but it still wasn't the worst thing that happened in band.

The final act of bullying was so nasty it caused both of my kids to quit. One day during practice, two girls yelled across the entire band, "Hey Nick, are you gay?" When Nick responded no, they laughed. "We find that hard to believe!" Then some of the other band kids joined in mocking Nick. He came home from school so upset his bottom lip quivered as he cried and told me about it. My heart hurt seeing his spirit so crushed. I asked him if I could call the mother of one of the girls because I knew her, although not very well.

I called the mother to tell her about her daughter's bullying and practically begged her to instruct her children, who were all in band, to not tell anyone at school that we spoke. She kindly assured me they wouldn't say anything.

I had not intervened for Nick like that since I talked to that one little third grader in front of the school many years earlier.

Before I called, Nick and I discussed the possibility that he might get grief over it from the band kids the next day, but we were desperate to make the bullying stop. Unfortunately, the risk did not pay off and calling the mom just made matters worse, making both my kids so fed up they decided to quit.

When I called the band director to tell him Nick and Kelli were dropping out of band, he felt terrible. He was shocked and said he had no idea Nick was being bullied during practice. He encouraged me to have my kids stay in the program and kindly offered to talk to the whole group about it. I politely shot down that idea because that would just make matters worse for Nick. If my call to that mother triggered those kids to give Nick more grief, I could only imagine what a lecture from the band director would do. I explained Nick and Kelli had already made up their minds to quit, but I wanted him to understand just how bad it had been for my son. Maybe then he could stop those kids from picking on another student in the future. I also shared how Nick was told by one boy during marching practice to go kill himself. At that, the director was at a loss for words other than to say he understood.

More Bullying

Kelli recently told me about another time in high school when she saw one of Nick's classmates ridicule her brother. Nick was sitting in the hallway eating a banana when this kid accused him of being gay and insinuated all kinds of things about him and the banana. He shouted these things to Nick across a crowded hallway and humiliated him in front of his peers.

I'm sure Nick had to deal with this type of behavior all the time. To some of these kids, all that mattered was that *they* thought he was gay. They were trying to "out" him, regardless of his feelings, or even if it was true. Why do people of all ages think it's okay to accuse someone of being gay, make fun of gays, or try to "out" someone? All of this is bullying, period.

As I was writing this chapter, I read in my Google News feed that a nine-year-old boy from Denver took his life after being bullied for "coming out" to his classmates.[1] In colleges, there is an impactful educational movement to teach young men that "no means no." There needs to be a similar nationwide push to teach middle school, high school, and college students that it is wrong to make fun of someone's sexuality and to try to "out" someone. Maybe we could mandate that kids learn about topics, like sexual orientation and gender identity, as part of the sex education classes that most kids have to take in school.

After hearing about that nine-year-old, I think these lessons can start as early as grade school—in an age-appropriate way, of course. Too many people who have suffered this type of cruelty have killed themselves, and I believe it was a contributing factor in Nick's suicide. We all have to work together to be more accepting of others and must teach our kids how to do that from a very young age.

Graduation Party and Friends?

As Nick's high school years were coming to a close, he looked forward to graduating and going off to college, but he knew he first had to get through his graduation party. He was dreading it. The mere thought of a party made him anxious because he feared no kids would show up. From the time Nick was a little boy, he never wanted a birthday party for the same reason. Every time we offered to throw him one, he politely declined, no matter how much we tried to talk him into it. He used to celebrate his birthday with his sister and a few other girls in the neighborhood, but there was never a group of little boys to invite—only one boy, one time.

Nick was turning six or seven, and a boy who lived in our neighborhood came out to lunch with us. Throughout the entire meal, Nick anxiously kept trying to take a book out of his coat pocket to read because he was having such a hard time talking to him. Later that day, I explained to Nick the social etiquette of making a guest feel welcome. As I sat with him, I got a real sense of the pressure Nick felt that day trying to make conversation with the boy.

At that age, he was not used to talking one-on-one with boys. His sister, cousins, and the few friends he had were all girls. Anytime he tried to hang out with boys in the neighborhood or at school, it didn't go very well. They wanted to play ball, but Nick was not athletically inclined. All he wanted to do was talk about planes. His interests were so different, creating a distance between him and the boys his age. His passion for his interests seemed peculiar to most of them, which only widened the gap even more. Over time, that distance turned into exclusion and isolation.

Now so many years later, I fought hard to hold back my tears as Nick sat at the kitchen table once again stressing over what should have been a happy event. He held the high school phone directory in hand and called classmate after classmate sweating out whether anyone would willingly show up for his graduation party. I'm not sure how many kids Nick invited, but it was a lot. Although he didn't say so, he was anxious up to the day of his party—we all were.

Thank God, Nick had a pretty decent turnout of friends, family, and neighbors with about fifteen kids showing up. Most of the friends who attended were girls, but there were a few guys there too. It was a lovely gathering that meant more to Nick than words can ever describe. I will go so far as to say it brightened his spirits after four long—often difficult—years of high school and was a pleasant closure for that period in his life.

The summer between graduation and college, Nick told us, once again, that he was growing tired of coming up empty-handed in the friend department. As in years past, we saw him repeatedly try to make plans with those three guys I talked about earlier, as well as a few others, to no avail. Nick wanted a best friend other than his sister. Sure, he appreciated the female friends he had from his graduating class, but he wanted some guy friends. He wanted buddies. In all of Nick's years, there were only one or two times that a boy came to the house to hang out with him. Now that he had graduated from high school, he was reflecting on his childhood, and I think it was really bothering him that he never had close male friendships. He was sad and lonely.

Lunch Date before College—Where Do I Fit in the World?

Right before Nick went to college, he made plans to go out to lunch with a girl from his graduating class who was beautiful inside and out. He thought the world of her, and she of him. They seemed to like each other and even went to one of the formal dances together in high school; however, I don't think their lunch was a date. They were getting together as friends one last time before going their separate ways for college.

When Nick came home from their lunch, he stood next to me in the kitchen and began to cry. It was like someone opened the floodgates. He was doing "the ugly cry," which I had not seen him do since he was a little boy. He told me she was the perfect girl: intelligent, beautiful, and funny. She had everything any guy would ever want. He was upset because he felt he should be attracted to her romantically but wasn't and could not understand why. Nick wiped his tears and said he was afraid he could never love a woman, even though he wanted to so badly. I hugged him and told him it was okay but could tell this was not giving him much comfort. He said all he wanted was a normal life. I tried to give him hope by telling him he could have a happy and loving relationship with whomever he decided in life, male or female. Nick told me he wasn't attracted to guys in that way either, so he didn't think he was gay.

My son was hurting so much and was so confused. I racked my brain, trying to figure out what I could say and what he needed to hear from me that would help him. I wanted to make it better like I had done so many times when he was younger, but he was struggling with things that were way bigger and more complex now. I knew that loving him and telling him things would work out just wasn't enough, but that was all I had right then. My heart was breaking as I tried to assure him that he just needed time to figure things out for himself.

In that same conversation, Nick brought up the topic of "closeted" men who marry women, have kids, and conceal their true sexual orientation from them. Nick said he would feel like he was living a lie and could never do that to his family. I tried to comfort him by telling him he was just eighteen and did not have to figure it all out right then. Poor Nick was having an internal battle, and I didn't know what more to say except that I loved him for who he was, and if he were confused now, then I would also love and accept him later when he figured it all out—no matter what.

It is extremely difficult for me to write about any of this because it was a very private conversation between us about a very personal topic; however, Tom, Kelli, and I have decided we should share Nick's struggle because a lot of people, like him, are confused about their sexual orientation. We *know* he would want us to write and talk about what he was going through if it could somehow help others because he was selfless and had a generous heart. We are honoring Nick by sharing his story.

Sexual orientation (who you like) and gender identity (what you feel on the inside) are private and not open for discussion, unless a person wants to talk about it—and then it should be done on that individual's terms. We need to teach kids about privacy, tolerance, inclusion, compassion, and respect at a very young age. Nick was born a male, identified as being male, and was not questioning his gender identity; however, he was confused about his sexual orientation (who he liked). Nick questioned whether he was gay, straight, or asexual (experiencing little or no sexual attraction to others and/or lack of interest in sexual relationships or behavior). Although many other sexual orientations exist, these are the three Nick questioned about himself.

Based on all our conversations with Nick, and through the benefit of hindsight, Tom, Kelli, and I believe he loved everyone but was not sexually or romantically attracted to any gender. We think he was asexual, although none of us understood much about it when Nick was alive. He was confused and frustrated about not being able to feel sexual attraction toward others. I think when Nick discovered he wasn't attracted to females, he, like the rest of us, just assumed that meant he was gay. On television and in the movies, men who aren't attracted to females are portrayed as being gay. There is, however, never any talk about asexuality. Throughout middle school, high school, and college, kids either asked Nick if he was gay, assumed he was gay, or insinuated he was gay through snide remarks. All of this added to his doubts and frustration.

Then, as Nick discovered he wasn't attracted to men, he grew even more confused and would tell us that he thought he was straight. He kept flip-flopping. Later, Nick clarified that he didn't seem to be attracted to females *or* males. He loved everyone but was romantically attracted to no one. Perhaps this would have changed over time, as well.

In Nick's mind, he didn't know who he was, where he fit in, how he was supposed to live his life, or when it would all get better. He had no hope for a bright future. At least what Nick did know, without a doubt, was that his family accepted him for who he was and would *always* love him—unconditionally. We made a point of telling him so, over and over again. We just wanted him to be happy.

Although Nick often told us how much he appreciated our love and support, it was not enough for him to *stay*. I believe his struggles with sexual orientation, together with his history of rejection, not fitting in, and bullying, either caused or contributed to a mental health issue. It all compounded his anguish, eventually causing him to take his life. We will never know for sure whether Nick was straight, gay, asexual, or any other sexual orientation, and it is a moot point except to use his struggles to help others.

Some people, like Nick, may feel hopeless and even suicidal because they are confused and unable to figure out their sexual orientation and/or gender identity. Others may know these things but perhaps don't want to live outside of what's typically considered the "norm" in society. If you are having difficulties with sexual orientation, gender identity, both, or anything else, I'm sure Nick would want me to tell you to please give your struggles time to work themselves out. These things may take time to understand, so know that not immediately having all the answers is all right. The world has lost too many beautiful souls for these reasons. Please *stay*. Life is always worth living. What seems impossible today will get better with the benefit of some time.

Back in 2013, when Nick was questioning, information about sexual orientation and gender identity was not as readily available as it is now. Since then, thankfully, many more individuals have bravely come forward to share their stories all over social media and everywhere else to help people who are questioning or struggling with their sexual orientation and/or identity. Look to these resources to learn how life got better for these individuals. Some of their struggles may be relatable to your own. They will tell you, as I am now, to give it time and hang on. Also, there are websites and resources that explain the various sexual orientations and gender identities. The resources page on the Nick's Network of Hope website (nicksnetworkofhope.org), a site I created for people to get information and resources about certain life challenges, lists a few of those many websites that address these issues. I discuss more about Nick's Network of Hope in chapter 14.

We are continually making progress with acceptance and rights in our country, and we need everyone here to *stay* and help teach tolerance and kindness. We are all God's children, and He loves us all equally—no exception. Do not let anyone tell you, or make you think, otherwise.

COLLEGE

As college approached, Nick got more and more excited about having another opportunity to make new friends. He was clinging to hope. In hindsight, I believe Nick was thinking this was his last chance at making friends, and he was going to try his best to give it one more chance.

I already talked about what happened when Nick got to college—the rumor about his sexuality, the freshmen guys who treated him like he was invisible, the private residence with strange rules, and the guys who strung Nick along without signing an apartment lease. All this weighed heavily on Nick and wore him down. College was his last hope for making lasting friendships, but after a year of being excluded by certain friend groups, becoming the victim of a rumor, not knowing his sexual orientation, and not knowing where he fit in, Nick gave up. I think he felt like an outsider who had been rejected by almost everyone. Nick knew he had a loving family, but he believed the world would be better off without him because, in his mind, he was nothing more than a burden. The two hate videos posted by his peers represent what he had to endure throughout his nineteen years.

Chapter 9

Stigma and Complexities
of Mental Health

Stigma: A mark of disgrace associated with a
particular circumstance, quality, or person.

—Lexico.com

There are times it would be easier for our whole family to hide the fact that Nick killed himself, but we can't. When a loved one dies from suicide, it's a little like wearing your worst underwear on the outside of your pants, or even on your head, for the world to see. Mental health issues and suicide are out there in front of everyone to examine and judge. Sure, people can sell their homes, relocate, and try to lay low by talking to as few people as possible, but human beings aren't wired to be antisocial, and this would just compound their unhappiness. People can attempt to run from it, but they cannot hide, no matter how hard they try. There is no covering up, and there is no way to make it appear better because people will eventually learn the truth, especially with the advent of the internet. Between social media and newspapers, word of Nick's suicide spread almost instantly.

Mental health issues and suicide are things people cannot dress up or camouflage. The only thing covering them is pain and stigma, which attaches to everyone. Let me explain. A person contemplating suicide has to handle the pain and stigma connected to his or her mental health issue(s). If that person dies by suicide, then upon death, the pain and stigma morph and attach to the survivors. That is a difficult thing for survivors to accept, especially when they are trying to grasp the fact their loved one just died by suicide.

The pain all suicide loss survivors suffer eventually lessens as people heal, although it never goes away entirely due to the permanence of the loss. The stigma, on the other hand, does not seem to lessen at all. At least it hasn't in my experience. It just hangs out there and seems to have a life of its own. How people react and adapt to it varies from person to person. I have seen people try to avoid the stigma entirely and attempt to cover up their loved one's suicide by telling people it was an accident. Others try to pretend it did not happen at all.

Not too long ago, I met with a mother about ten days after her seventeen-year-old daughter hanged herself. Her other teenage daughter was with us as we sat and talked about what they were feeling and what they could expect in the future as they grieved. I offered the mother tips about what I usually do when someone asks me how many kids I have (see chapter 10). Much to my surprise, and even more to her daughter's, the mother said if anyone were to ask how many children she has, she planned to answer two, not three, because the third child was the one who died by suicide, and it would just be easier to not even mention her.

Every parent who has lost a child to suicide can relate to this woman wanting to avoid the stigma, but I think to deny the suicide ever happened or, worse yet, that a loved one even existed only delays the healing process. It seems to me that even if people try to cover up mental health issues and suicide, outsiders will most likely learn the truth, leaving the family to look like liars or, at the very least, as not being forthright. Also, if the loss survivors are parents who have other children, they need to consider what message they are sending their kids when they try to cover up the suicide. Aren't they indirectly saying that if something terrible also happens to them, they will deny their existence as well? Or if life gets too demanding, it is acceptable to lie to everyone? It's easier to lose your reputation for honesty and respect from your kids than it is to hide from stigma.

This mother had just buried her daughter the week before we spoke. I bet she later changed her mind about not wanting to mention that daughter to others. She was probably still in shock, and her response was more of a quick answer without having time to think it all through. I know for sure I was not thinking straight the second week after Nick died. I admire her for having the courage to sit down with me and talk about her daughter's suicide so soon after it happened.

Mental health issues are nothing to be ashamed of, and we have to keep reminding ourselves of that. Would we try to cover up an illness that was physical instead of mental? Not normally, right? We do not try to hide someone's leukemia or kidney disease, yet often people feel the need to cover up mental illness. Many suffering from depression try to hide it from their families and friends for fear of being thought of as "crazy," or worse yet, being treated like it. Some fear they will lose their jobs or be passed over for promotions if their employers find out about their mental health issues.

It's a shame we have to be so afraid to admit when someone has a mental health condition or when a suicide happens, or is attempted. Why does stigma arise and attach in the first place? Stigma is created because the ranges of the issues are wide and the issues themselves can be very complex. We don't know as much about illnesses that are psychological and tend to judge those things we are ignorant about or don't understand. There is so much unknown about our brains, but as part of our bodies, they can get broken and sick like any other part. Just as there is a whole range of physical illnesses from colds to cancers, there is also an entire range of mental illnesses, from depression to more significant ones like dissociative mental disorder (previously known as multiple personality disorder) and schizophrenia.

Many times, the general public is not even sure what terms to use to describe when something goes off-kilter in our brains. We call it a mental health illness, condition, disorder, problem, or issue. All these terms are used interchangeably in society. Unfortunately, there is a subjective amount of stigma attached to each of these terms, causing some people to prefer one or more over another. It took me a few years to feel comfortable calling my son's issue a "mental illness." Somehow, calling it a mental health condition or issue was easier for me, emotionally. Whenever I thought of mental illness, only severe ones like schizophrenia came to mind. I had to remind myself that there is a whole spectrum of mental illness, which includes depression. Now I use all the terms interchangeably when referring to Nick. The bottom line is that you should use whatever words make you feel most comfortable, but try not to get caught up in semantics. The stigma surrounding all these terms will lessen the more we use each of them. Throughout this book, I have used these terms interchangeably to help lift the stigma attached to each one.

Another reason stigma surrounds mental health issues is that problems of the mind can be so complex that their onsets are difficult to recognize. Some symptoms of mental health conditions are obvious, but others can be very difficult to recognize when they begin to surface. Maybe a person has had an issue since birth, or perhaps it developed during the teenage years. Some people may be mentally healthy their whole lives and develop mental health issues during old age or as a result of trauma. Perhaps they endured physical illnesses or environmental stressors that caused mental health issues to develop. A mental health problem could exist for years or come on instantaneously, like a mental break.

A lawsuit filed by a family in my hometown exemplifies how someone could have a sudden mental break from excessive fear and distress. According to the *Chicago Tribune*, the lawsuit alleged two high school deans and a police officer assigned to the school questioned a sixteen-year-old high school junior about recording his consensual, sexual encounter with a female classmate on his cell phone that he had played for friends. The lawsuit further alleged that these school officials accused the boy of possessing child pornography (the recording turned out to be audio only) and threatened him about having to register as a sex offender with the state. The boy was questioned for eighteen minutes before his mother was called.

The officials stopped the meeting while the mother was in transit to the school, and the teen was told to sit in a waiting area by some administrative offices. He complied but slipped away minutes later, walked downtown, and jumped off a five-story municipal parking garage about a mile from the school.[1] The coroner's report indicated the teen had no history of mental illness or suicide ideation, otherwise known as thoughts of suicide.[2]

A federal judge dismissed the lawsuit (the parents appealed then later settled the case[3]) and opined that the defendants' questioning of the boy constituted ordinary police interrogation tactics. In her ruling, the judge stated, "Faced with the implied threat of such consequences, it is perhaps unsurprising that a previously well-adjusted teenager's emotional state could deteriorate to such a point that he would contemplate taking his life."[4] A mental health issue seemed to occur instantaneously in this instance, but many times, it can be difficult to know when an issue begins.

I have no idea when my son's illness started, and I don't know if he had more than one. I am also clueless about how his mental condition was progressing, if at all. I do know, however, that it was much more debilitating than we realized because it led to his suicide. Our family will never get answers to all our questions, and that is something we have learned to accept.

The nature of Nick's illness was not apparent and fooled a lot of people, even his own family. Every member of our extended family was shocked when Nick took his life. They told me over and over again how they had no idea he was struggling. Many of the notes written by Nick's classmates in his high school yearbook mention how Nick was always so happy and often had a big smile on his face, which makes me believe his classmates also didn't know how badly he was hurting.

Tom and I spoke with Alex and Jerry, Nick's two friends in college. They, too, said they never saw anything in Nick that made them think he had a mental health issue. Friends and neighbors repeatedly told us how Nick seemed so confident and looked like he had his "act together," and some even commented that he was the last kid they thought would ever take his life. So how did his mental illness stay under the radar and fool so many people for so long, including two trained psychologists who agreed he showed no signs of being at risk for suicide?

The complex nature of mental health truly gives life to the stigma surrounding it: the not always knowing what mental health issues look like, the frequent difficulties in recognizing when mental health issues develop, and the not understanding what terms to use when referring to mental health issues. Now add to that our tendency to jump to conclusions and judge things we do not fully understand, and the stigma surrounding mental health festers.

It is frustrating that stigma attaches to mental health issues, suicide attempts, suicides, suicide attempt survivors, and suicide loss survivors, but it does and will continue to do so until we all start talking openly about mental health. If you are painfully familiar with this stigma, how do you handle it? We do have control over what we do with the stigma once it attaches. Do we let it silence us, or do we open up and talk about it to anyone who will listen so that in our lifetime we will hopefully see that stigma diminish? We absolutely can change how people perceive mental health issues if we keep talking about them.

If you have a mental illness, do not be ashamed. It is important to get the help you need. Then if you are ready, willing, and able to do so without it negatively affecting your health, talk about your mental health issues. If you are a suicide loss survivor, you too should never feel ashamed. I encourage you to go out and talk about what happened, provided doing so will not hurt you psychologically or cause a setback in your healing. The more we share, the more we all can learn about mental health and get used to viewing it without judgment, like we do physical health. You are not disrespecting your loved one by opening up and talking about his or her issue. Do not let the stigma that is present in today's society paralyze you from healing or from possibly trying to help someone else. We must combat the misconceptions some people have about those who struggle and die by suicide. You can make a difference. I am hopeful we can destigmatize mental health issues if we all do our part.

MISCONCEPTION ABOUT SELFISHNESS

Sometimes when people hear about a suicide attempt, they are quick to judge the person suffering from a mental health problem. By talking more about our struggles and those of our loved ones and friends, we can combat this stigma and eradicate these misconceptions.

Some people think those who attempt suicide act selfishly because they believe the attempt is a choice to leave their friends and family behind, making them suffer the consequences of their deaths. This is a common misconception about those who attempt, whether they survive or not.

About a month after Nick passed, I had a very close friend tell me she was mad at him for everything he put our family through with his choice. She thought it was an incredibly selfish thing to do. Her opinion was difficult for me to hear, but I wasn't mad. I told her there were a few moments when I felt angry with Nick for leaving, but then I quickly reminded myself how much pain he endured. Never for a moment did I think his suicide was a selfish act. In fact, throughout his life, he acted quite oppositely and was the most selfless person I have ever known. I tried to explain to her that Nick was in such excruciating mental anguish he just wanted to make the pain stop. He wasn't putting himself before Tom, Kelli, or me. I explained what he was going through, but it's just difficult for people to imagine that level of pain if they do not have a mental illness or have never lived with someone who has.

The following metaphors for the amount of pain and desperation people feel pale in comparison to reality, but stay with me here. If you had a huge grand piano fall on your chest and could not breathe, would you be thinking about your mother, sister, or friend? No. Your only thoughts would be, "I need to breathe! Get this piano off my chest!" You would do *anything* to get it off, right? Have you ever had a piece of food lodged in your throat so badly you thought you might die? This recently happened to me. As I was choking, I was not thinking about my family or the huge man who was doing the Heimlich on me who easily could have broken my ribs. I could think of only one thing, "I need oxygen!" And I would have done anything to get it.

People who attempt suicide, whether they die from it or not, are in crippling pain and will do *anything* to make it stop—even end their lives. I will never forget what our parish priest said about Nick's state of mind when he visited Tom, Kelli, and me a few days after Nick died. I asked him point-blank if he thought Nick was in heaven. I believed my son was there and figured he thought so too, but I was curious *how* he would respond. His answer gave me much comfort. He said, "Yes, it takes a lot to jump from a bridge." It was comforting that he recognized how much pain and mental anguish Nick was suffering when he stood on that bridge and jumped.

It also "takes a lot" to do things like jump from a municipal parking garage, shoot yourself in the head, put a noose around your neck, or take a handful of pills. In each of these cases, the person is suffering from an incredible amount of pain. The pain is so intense and debilitating they cannot think about anyone or anything. They only want their pain to end. Their action is one of desperation, not selfishness or disrespect.

Then what about people who leave a suicide note? They are able to think of their families and friends, right? Yes, for a brief moment, but while in anguish and with pianos on their chests or food lodged in their throats, unable to breathe. The note exemplifies how much they loved them, not how much they were thinking of themselves.

MISCONCEPTION ABOUT COWARDICE

People never directly told me they thought Nick's suicide was cowardly, though they may have said it behind my back. I have heard this said about other suicides, as well as things like, "That person gave up instead of doing the hard work to get better," or "They took the easy way out by killing themselves." Whenever I hear something like that, it frustrates me. If we think about all the different ways people end their own lives, none of them exactly shout out, "This was the easy way out." Going to therapy, changing a medication, trying a new treatment, or anything else would be easier. Calling people who are suffering from mental anguish "cowards" is insensitive—period.

MISCONCEPTION ABOUT LACK OF FAITH IN HIGHER POWER

When I was writing this chapter, the designer Kate Spade and the celebrity chef Anthony Bourdain died by suicide. I read many articles posted to my Google News feed by people weighing in on what they thought causes suicide. It seems many people outside the mental health field feel the need to share their opinions whenever celebrities take their lives. The one article that frustrated me the most was by a female blogger who said that people who take their own lives are not cowards or selfish (good so far), they just lack faith in God. Seriously?

I do not condone suicide; however, this woman's theory is just wrong in regard to most suicides. I am a woman of faith and agree it is always best to put trust in God if you have the mental capacity to do so. There are people in this world who believe in a higher power, while others do not. It is the same with people who take their lives—during their lives, some were believers, and some were not. But for those believers who died by suicide, in most cases, they did not take their own lives because they no longer believed in or trusted in God. They had severe mental health issues or had some kind of instantaneous mental break and were in extreme pain. Although they exercised free will, they lacked the mental capacity to be responsible for it. Trying to stop the pain and anguish from a crippling mental illness or break does not equal a lack of faith. It just doesn't. For this woman to make a blanket statement and say all people who take their lives do so because they lack faith in God is just shortsighted and insensitive.

I know for a fact that Nick had very strong faith, and I have spoken with many loss survivor families who told me that their loves ones also had a solid faith. They had pianos on their chests, not a lack of faith. This woman's opinion is further proof that people who have not experienced a severe mental illness, first- or secondhand, have a difficult time understanding or relating to people who do. Opinions like hers add to the stigma around mental health issues and suicide.

There is so much we do not know when it comes to mental health. When people don't understand something, they tend to make judgments about it and form misconceptions resulting in stigma around that topic. The more people talk about mental health issues and suicide, the more educated and familiar we will become with these matters, which will result in less ignorance. With less ignorance about these subjects, fewer people will make judgments and form misconceptions. We are making progress in our efforts to reduce stigma and will continue to do so if we all continue to talk to one another about mental health.

Chapter 10

Social Landmines

GOING OUT FOR GROCERIES

Our social interactions became more difficult after Nick died, mostly due to the stigma that attached to his death and all of us after his suicide. You may be wondering how to talk with someone going through a significant loss like ours, or perhaps you are the one trying to get out there and talk with people again. Maybe someone you know lost a loved one to suicide, and you are frustrated because they can never seem to "get over it." They refuse to talk to anyone about it and prefer to stay home all the time.

Hopefully, by sharing how we went from not wanting to leave our house to being able to discuss Nick's death somewhat comfortably, it will help others. The following is one detailed and up-close example of what suicide loss survivors go through when trying to get back into society. It was a process for sure, but if we could make it back into the world socializing and interacting with people again, so can others.

At first, we did not want to walk out our front door, but at some point, we had to get groceries. We held our breath the whole time we shopped, hoping we would not run into anyone we knew who would stop and ask us a bunch of questions. I also started noticing the "complainers" in life. These are people who always gripe about small, petty things. I became almost hypersensitive to them and noticed they were everywhere. I never realized how many people in the Midwest complain about the weather to cashiers during checkout—and not just during nasty weather. I'm ashamed to admit this, but at first, there was a small part of me that wanted to shock-and-awe them and yell, "Rain is not a problem. Having your kid jump from a bridge—now *that's* a problem!"

It took me a few years before complainers stopped irritating me so much. I had to realize I was the one who was no longer normal after what we had gone through. I had an altered perspective, whereas the "complainers" were just going along living their lives. Sure, it is good not to sweat the small stuff, but I had to cut people slack when they did. And by the way, after a few years, I started to complain about some smaller stuff too every now and then, which was a sure sign of healing.

Our grieving was intertwined with our social encounters on every level. We could not control it or limit it to times when we were home alone because there was no on-off switch. If we were awake, we were grieving, and no matter how much we tried to act normal, people could see it. We were just not the same as we used to be. And it never failed—it seemed like every time I was out, I ran into someone who asked me straight up what happened to Nick. Even if they didn't ask, sometimes I felt like I still had to offer some explanation, and that never went well. I was bobbing and weaving through social landmines every time I left the house. The hardest part, though, was that I was still processing and trying to figure out for myself what happened, making it difficult to answer questions or offer explanations about how Nick died.

The responses seemed to change a little each day as I thought more about what happened and looked at it in different ways. If Nick's heart had stopped on a basketball court, then explaining what happened to him would have been more black-and-white, but with suicide, there are so many unanswered questions. Even my answer to the most basic question, "How are you?" changed from day to day. One day I would tell someone I was doing pretty well and believed it. Then, the very next day, if I were weepy-eyed and feeling especially down, I would feel like a complete fraud for having told someone that I was all right just a day earlier.

Grieving is one heck of a process. It is not linear and has no pattern. And it is true: grief does come in waves. If you are in the middle of having a good day, you still hold on tight because you know the very next wave is going to hit soon—you just don't know when. The good news is that, except for holidays, birthdays, and anniversaries of the passing, the time in between waves gets longer each year.

FIRST STEPS BACK INTO SOCIETY: TALKING WITH OTHER SCHOOL PARENTS

When it first happened, we did not go out socially, except when we had no choice. Kelli was in high school, so Tom and I had to attend a few school functions as her parents, like picture parties before school dances, parent-teacher conferences, and school Masses. Kelli was on the tennis team, so we conversed with other parents while watching her games from the bleachers. All the other parents were very kind to us and gave us a lot of support, which we really appreciated, but talking to them brought up all kinds of emotions.

When they updated us about their kids, we felt **sad** because we would never be able to talk about what Nick was doing ever again. We felt **lonely and misunderstood** because we knew no one could understand that we would never feel as carefree as them. Interestingly, we were **not envious** of what they had, but were somehow more **aware** of it and recognized the value. Whenever we heard people complaining about their kids, we felt almost **protective** of their relationships and wanted to tell them to stop, go home, and hug them. A few people looked at us with compassionate pity, which made us feel a little **self-conscious**, but we understood. We also felt **relief** because these parents knew about Nick's suicide before we even sat down to talk with them, so we did not have to be bearers of bad news repeatedly. I'm sure their kids came home from school and told them the day after it happened because news travels quickly in a small high school. We were **comforted** that these parents knew Nick and what type of person he was because then they had a pretty good understanding of our loss.

As time went on, we had to start going back to our daily lives, which meant we had to go out more and more. This took a lot of our energy because each time we saw people who had not yet heard what happened, we had to tell them. We had no choice but to talk about Nick's suicide over and over again with our eye doctor, dentist, medical doctor, hairstylist, dog groomer, veterinarian, long-distance friends, business associates, and everyone else. These people usually asked us about our kids, so we had to break it to them the next time we saw them. Each time we retold Nick's story, it weighed on us and was shocking and uncomfortable for others to hear.

DIFFICULT SOCIAL INTERACTIONS WITH FRIENDS

Even conversations with *good* friends and people who already knew what happened could be difficult. Let's go back to the example I used earlier of my good friend telling me she thought

Nick's last act was selfish. It took a lot for her to share with me that she was angry with him. After all, I was his mother. Only a good friend could say something like that and know it would not affect our relationship. I appreciated her honesty and was not offended, even though I was taken aback by her comments. She was feeling this way only because she cared deeply about our family. I wanted to take her emotions into account but also wanted to defend my son because I did not agree he acted selfishly. It took some social finesse to balance these considerations, which ordinarily would not have been so difficult; however, Nick had just died some weeks earlier, and it was all I could do to just get out of bed and function. We did this type of social gymnastics all the time after Nick passed.

One of the most trying conversations I experienced took me completely by surprise. Someone I knew well asked me how far Nick floated down the river before his body was found. I cannot remember what my exact response was, but I do remember it was appropriately vague, decently polite, and required much restraint. I was never too sensitive about what people asked or said to me after Nick passed, but I have to admit, that question stunned me.

Another day a dear friend offered to take me to lunch as a kind gesture of support. Before we got out of her car in the restaurant parking lot, she told me she was seeing and hearing Nick all around me as I sat in her passenger seat. Her communications with Nick continued on and off throughout our entire lunch. Whether she had the ability to do that is not the point, it was just a lot to take in so soon after losing my child, especially when I was not expecting it. Her heart was in the right place, though.

VOLUNTARILY SOCIALIZING WITH OTHERS

As we continued to heal, Tom and I started to venture out and go to more social functions, even ones we did not have to attend. We still did not feel much like going out but knew we had to push ourselves to heal and assimilate back into life. It was not easy. Early on, some people hesitated to talk with us or even avoided us altogether. We noticed whenever people kept from striking up conversations with us and didn't take it personally because we figured they just didn't know what to say. Even now, seeing us sometimes reminds people that something as awful as losing a child could happen to them, and they do not want to think about that. When they drag their feet to come to talk to us or avoid us, I get it. They are out having a good time, and we are a reminder of something horrific. And if by some chance they are having difficulties with one of their kids, they want to approach us even less.

Just recently I went out to dinner with a good friend. At the end of the evening, she apologized for not being in touch with me for the last year or so. She was having a lot of difficulties with her son and did not want to see me for a while because it would have been too scary for her and a reminder of what could happen to him. She smiled and said her son was better now, so she felt like she could call me and get together again. Hearing that did not offend me whatsoever because I understood and told her so in hopes of making her feel better. It is, however, sad that I was the person who could evoke fear in her and be a reminder of something that would cause her pain. Seven years after losing Nick, I am still a reminder of suicide for people, and at this point, I believe I always will be.

Being the people who have experienced a loved one's death by suicide swings both ways, though. It can push people away because it reminds them of what could happen in their families, or it can draw them near because they want to learn more about our experience. Yes, some people actually seek us out because of what happened in our lives. They tell us about their child or someone else they know who has a mental health condition or took his or her life. Just about every week I receive phone calls from people wanting to talk about these issues. Tom and I are always willing to try to help people any way we can by listening to them and sharing our experience. People feel comfortable talking to us because they know we have already been through it and will listen without judgment.

I am happy to say I think even people who have not experienced significant challenges with mental illness and suicide feel pretty comfortable talking with us now, even though Nick's death sometimes comes up in conversation. How could it not? It is a fact of our lives and part of our history. And when it does, it can sometimes cause awkward moments in our conversations, like when we are all talking about the accomplishments of our kids. It can be uncomfortable for everyone. The people feel our loss, then we feel sad that they are feeling our loss, and then at that moment, we feel sad about our loss too—what a mess. Everyone is talking and having a good time, and then our *ping* gets felt by everyone in the conversation. There is a positive takeaway, though. Nick's death, like all suicides, reminds us all about what is important in life, how we should appreciate our friends and loved ones, how much kindness matters, and how precious our time is here.

MEETING NEW PEOPLE

Meeting people for the first time is an entirely different undertaking. It usually involves small talk like it does for everyone else in the world, except the conversation inevitably turns to something not too small. Typically, within the first five questions, we get asked *the* question: "So how many kids do you have?" Think about it—it is a question that almost always comes up in conversations unless you are single without kids or too young to have them. Early on, Tom and I used to tense up in anticipation of that question and cringe even more while trying to come up with an answer. I'm sure our body language screamed we were in discomfort and wanted to run. At first, we would answer, "We have two," and hoped they wouldn't ask any follow-up questions. They almost always did with, "How old are they?" That one little question, which seemed so harmless, was the point of no return because it forced us to go down the rabbit hole of telling the kind people we just met that our son passed away, making them feel uncomfortable. Then, after making it through answering that our son died, we used to think, "For the love of God, don't ask *how*." But sometimes they did.

Now seven years later, even though the questions coming from people we meet are still the same, they do not bother us nearly as much anymore. The questions remain somewhat uncomfortable, but we don't tense up like we used to. When people ask me how many kids we have, I now can look them straight in the eye and say, "Two: one here and one on the other side." The usual response is, "Oh, I'm sorry." Then I typically say, "That's okay. We lost our son to suicide seven years ago." I say he died by suicide instead of having them wonder how he died and sparing them from having to contemplate if they should ask any follow-up questions. I appreciate it cannot be easy for them to hear we lost a child. Then, I very briefly share that Nick was a wonderful person because it gives me pleasure to do so. After addressing the death, I am freed to concentrate on sharing more about Kelli. It helps when people hear it happened seven years ago because they know the pain is not as raw.

Tom says one of the most challenging demands of returning to work after Nick died was answering the question, "How many kids do you have?" in a business setting. He similarly responds by saying two and then talks about Kelli briefly, adding we lost our son "tragically" seven years ago. He says typically, in business settings, there are no follow-up questions about Nick, only Kelli.

How did we get to the point where we could talk about it with others and answer questions with more ease? It just took time and practice. Through trial and error, we found the words that made us feel the most comfortable while keeping the needs of the listener in mind. Of course, having healed some over time also helped a lot with our delivery. Some days we are better at answering those questions than others.

It is important to note that having some difficulty talking about Nick's death and answering questions never completely goes away and always causes a *ping* in our hearts. I recently went to my thirty-year law school reunion, and while I was excited to see all my wonderful classmates and friends, I had to tell them what happened to Nick on a night when everyone was happy and enjoying each other's company. I had almost six years of practice telling people, yet it was still difficult.

Everyone must find his or her way of talking to people about the death of a loved one. There is no one-size-fits-all approach when trying to figure out how to get back out there and socialize. You will find what works best for you. Expect to have to push yourself out of your comfort zone, which is mostly a good thing because it fosters growth; however, make sure you know your limits for wherever you are in the grief process. Don't push yourself to get out there so quickly that you hinder your healing. Right after a suicide, it's okay to be a little selfish and isolate yourself to heal. Be able to say no when people try to get you to do things you are not quite ready to do yet. Also, keep in mind the people you encounter will not know what to say to you at times, so give them a break if they are standoffish for a while or say something awkward when they do engage with you. Try not to take it personally. People usually do care and mean well; however, sometimes they just don't know how to show it.

BEING JUDGED

Although I just said that people usually care, there will always be a few who will judge you. Tom and I would be kidding ourselves if we thought no one judged us over Nick's suicide. Judging others is an ugly part of human nature, and we all do it. Here is why I think people judge suicide survivors. Generally, people do not want to think suicide can ever occur in their lives. Parents especially are terrified to think that it could happen to *their* children, so when they hear about an attempt or a suicide, some use judgment to distance it as far away as they can from their own family lives. It is a fear-based reaction. I will use Nick's suicide to illustrate: They tell themselves suicide will never happen to their kids because they judge that Tom and I *were*, or *acted like*, X, Y, or Z as parents to Nick and assure themselves they are not like that or do not do that, so they comfort themselves into thinking suicide will never happen to their kids. Or they judge Nicolas *was*, or *acted like*, A, B, or C, and assure themselves their child is not like that or does not do that, so once again they tell themselves they do not have to worry about suicide happening to their children.

I used to worry that some people who didn't know us automatically condemned us as being bad parents because Nick took his life, but I don't waste my time even thinking about that anymore. I cannot control what others think of my family, or me. In our hearts, we know we were good parents. We made our fair share of mistakes, just like everyone else, but we always put our kids first and tried 110 percent. If anyone wants to judge us without knowing us, then so be it. We can take it. We've been through a lot worse.

SIBLING OF SUICIDE

I want to take time to discuss what happened to our daughter after Nick's suicide because there may be other young people reading this who are struggling after losing a sibling. Kelli, of course, was completely broken up when she learned what happened to her big brother. She beat herself up over not recognizing Nick was suicidal, just like Tom and I did. She knew he was unhappy going to the University of Minnesota and even talked to him over Christmas break about possibly transferring to Purdue or DePaul the following year. They spoke about both of them attending DePaul in two years because that was one of the colleges Kelli was considering.

Kelli and Nick called and texted each other on and off throughout his entire first year of college and spent as much time together as they could when he came home for his winter and spring breaks. Unfortunately, Nick's spring break from college did not coincide with Kelli's. She had to go to school that week, cutting into their time together; nevertheless, they did hang out after she got home from classes. It was an unusually busy time at our home that week because their grandmother was in the hospital.

As a side note: My mother needed surgery to place a graft in her arm (a port to receive kidney dialysis) and then have her first dialysis treatment in the hospital. All week I needed to be by her side during the day. This weighed on me because I also wanted to spend time with Nick, especially after everything he had been going through at school. Poor Kelli wanted to spend time with Nick *and* her grandmother, but she had to go to school every day. Nick stayed home alone until Kelli got out of classes. It wasn't the optimum plan, but we all thought it best not to risk Nick getting sick by having him inside a hospital all week. Also, we figured it would have been emotionally draining on him to see his grandmother in kidney failure. His spring break was supposed to be a week of relaxation and a break from a tough semester, not more stress. Nick, however, did come to the hospital the day of Grandma's first dialysis treatment because he wanted to be there to show his support. Nick was a sensitive young man, but I found it a little strange when he cried most of the car ride home from the hospital. I attributed his emotions to seeing his grandmother hooked up to a dialysis machine, but in hindsight, I think Nick cried because he planned on taking his life soon, and he realized he had just seen his beloved Grandma for the very last time.

When Nick returned to Minnesota after spring break, he texted Kelli to tell her he was having trouble getting that group of guys to sign an apartment lease with him for the following school year. She consoled him like she often did and understood he was unhappy, but Kelli never thought he was suicidal because she had grown used to him having a hard time fitting in with other kids.

Throughout their school years together, Nick and Kelli spent many evenings sitting around in each other's rooms talking about what happened in school that day. Nick would often confide in her about what some of his classmates had said or done to him, which would often leave Kelli sick at heart and sometimes even angry. They were best friends who always looked out for each other. Kelli was one of Nick's most significant sources of support, but now that he was away at college, she could no longer see him every day.

Kelli was busy being a typical teenager concentrating on her own life's events, like friends, high school, and extracurricular activities. The last few days before Nick passed, Kelli knew Nick was telling Tom and me that he was having a tough weekend, but she did not understand just how bad it was for him. Many teenagers live in drama, so how was she to know that this time was something much, much more? How could Kelli possibly have imagined what was ahead? Like the rest of us, she had a hard time forgiving herself for not realizing how much Nick was suffering or that he was suicidal.

In an instant, Kelli lost her brother and closest friend, forever. She can no longer have those late-night talks with him about kids at school or people they like. She can no longer dream about their future doing things together like traveling, raising kids, and going to events. She can no longer laugh with him about how Tom and I said something embarrassing, didn't understand one of their inside jokes, or mispronounced some celebrity's name. He was the only person in the world who shared the same family and childhood experiences with her. Kelli will tell you that you cannot appreciate what all that means until you don't have that person anymore. With one leap, she became an only child and *our* only child in this physical world.

Kelli was finishing up her junior year when Nick died. She didn't take more than a few days off from school to mourn because her college preparatory school was fast-paced, and all her classes were challenging. I think she also wanted to return right away so she wouldn't have to make up time over the summer.

When Kelli went back to school, she began realizing that other high school students, and even friends who graduated and moved on to college, immediately felt comfortable telling her about their problems because of what happened to Nick. She started getting texts and late-night phone calls from kids who were having all kinds of difficulties, even a few who told her they were having thoughts of suicide. I imagine they thought she suddenly could understand more than most kids their age about these types of problems.

Late one evening, Tom and Kelli had to go to a boy's house to talk with his parents after he confided in her that he thought about killing himself. What these kids did not understand was that even though Kelli was empathetic, she was not in any position to be able to help them. She was just a teenager and was going through her own hell from losing her brother. The last thing Kelli needed was to have more put on her shoulders. She was grieving, living at home with two parents in mourning, doing her best to keep up at school, and trying to wrap her brain around the fact she was going to live the rest of her life without her brother—and add to that the typical day-to-day drama in the life of any teenager. There was no way she was qualified to help anyone with psychological or emotional issues.

Then, in the summer before her senior year, Kelli's grieving appeared to go away. She looked like she was picking up and getting on with her life, almost as if nothing ever happened. It helped that Kelli had a lot of friends in high school, a tight group of close girlfriends who supported her, and a grief counselor who was helping her work through her grief. But still, her "recovery" seemed a little too sudden. Tom and I were stumped about what was going on with her.

A few years later, Tom found two newsletter articles put out by the people at LOSS (**L**oving **O**utreach to **S**urvivors of **S**uicide—a nondenominational program created by Catholic Charities that supports individuals grieving the loss of a loved one by suicide) that helped explain Kelli's behavior. The newsletters said teenagers often delay some of their grieving and immerse themselves in their daily activities to cope with the loss because their young brains are generally incapable of handling a lot of trauma all at once.[1] That is exactly what Kelli had done. She grieved hard, initially, and then appeared to move past it too quickly. Without knowing it, she was doing precisely what was needed to heal by postponing some of her grief until she was a little older and better able to process it. Another Law of the Universe: grief never goes away until you work through it.

Kelli started college in the business school at the University of Illinois in 2014. During her freshman year, which was a year and a half after Nick's suicide, some of her grief started coming to the forefront again. Many times, she called home to say she was sad about not having her brother around. She understood that feeling these newly surfaced emotions meant she was ready to begin working through more of her grief.

I could somewhat relate to what Kelli was going through because I worked through delayed emotions as a teenager as well. My parents divorced when I was fifteen, and I pushed down some of my feelings for about four years. Then one chunk at a time, I worked through them when I was ready and able. Similar to Kelli's response, it was too overwhelming for me to try to handle the whole divorce at once, especially at that age. Divorce is not death, but I would imagine they are both traumatic to a young mind.

If you are reading this and your children have suffered a significant loss or some other trauma, please do not get upset if they appear not to be grieving appropriately or are showing fewer emotions than the rest of the family. Encourage them to see a counselor, let them talk through what happened, and be patient. When their emotions surface a little later, keep in mind that their grief is just as new to them now as yours was for you in the past.

So, during Kelli's freshman and sophomore years in college, she started grieving again and was faced with working through that grief while away at school. This was hard on her because although she had friends in college, she could not be home with her family and close girlfriends for emotional support. Tom and I often went to see her at school, and she came back for visits, but it was still tough for her to be two and a half hours away from us. Making matters worse, as she was trying to get a handle on this new grief, people at college were finding out her brother killed himself, and she had to deal with all the social effects of the stigma.

When Kelli first started at U of I, she was excited to meet people who didn't know anything about her past. It was refreshing that no one would see her as "the girl whose brother died by suicide." Kelli didn't want to hide that fact—she just wanted to pick and choose who she told and when she would tell them. She also wanted people to get to know her a little before they found out. Who could blame her for wanting people to meet her before the stigma?

Several graduates from Kelli's high school went to U of I, so word about Nick's suicide got out. Like all suicide loss survivors, Kelli had a difficult time getting in front of the gossip. Before freshman classes even started, she attended a party where all the new students were introducing themselves to one other. As Kelli walked around meeting people, she saw a girl from her high school across the room who had been talking with a group of other students. As Kelli walked over to meet them, she realized by the look on their faces that the girl had just told them what happened to Nick. Here Kelli had not even met them yet, and they knew the most complicated, trying, and private part of her life. That was how they were being introduced to her.

Kelli was getting hit with Nick's suicide from all angles. One student who was romantically interested in her tried to use the suicide to his advantage. He could tell his feelings for her were not mutual, so he tried to get Kelli to talk to him by telling her he had a vivid dream about her brother, whom he had never met. He said Nick gave him some messages for her. As Kelli put it, "What type of guy sinks so low as to use my dead brother to hit on me?"

My daughter has gone through a lot. I know I am biased because I'm her mother, but I am proud of her and think she has incredible strength. She endured so much in her young life, yet she still managed to work through a difficult grief journey. She graduated from a challenging business program at U of I, is currently working for a reputable law firm, and plans to attend law school within the year. Kelli has become a loving and compassionate young woman, all while keeping her standout sense of humor.

Chapter 11

More Grief and the New Family

EMOTIONS OF FIRST YEAR

n chapter 5, I talked about the first days of grief, as we walked around numb and in shock. We were not sleeping or eating much and felt like we were losing our minds. Nothing is as horrible as the first few days, but to be honest, the *entire* first year was like living through a hurricane. Waves of grief hit us without warning as we got batted around by a full range of emotions. The following are just some of the emotions our family experienced that first year. Each of us experienced different aspects of them in our own way, at different times, and for varying durations—but collectively, we hit them all.

Anger: Anger at Nick for not opening up and telling us he was having thoughts of suicide. Anger at God for letting Nick die. Anger at ourselves for missing warning signs. Anger at the world for continuing to go on when time seemed to stop for us.

Fear: Fear of forgetting some memories of Nick as we age. Fear of the unknown, and specifically of our new lives without Nick. Fear that one of us could get ill or drop dead from a heart attack from the extreme stress we were experiencing. Fear of getting back into the world. Fear the world would forget our son.

Hopelessness: Hopelessness in our future as we wondered if we would ever feel normal, truly happy, or pain-free again.

Regret: Regret for not realizing the extent of Nick's suffering. Regret from sending him to a college so far from home. Regret for not knowing all the risk factors and warning signs for suicide. Regret for sending him to class from Jamba Juice.

Sorrow: Sorrow in losing our future with Nick, as well as our hopes and dreams for his future. Sorrow that we would never see him in our physical world again—never hug or kiss him—never see him graduate, get his first job, get married, or have kids. Sorrow that Nick felt he was a burden and experienced so much pain. Sorrow for our daughter who lost her big brother and best friend.

Gratitude: Gratitude for the time we all shared. Gratitude for our faith and spirituality that carries us through the grief and helps us heal. Gratitude for our family and friends who were supporting and helping us work through our grief.

GRIEVING INDIVIDUALLY AND TOGETHER AS A FAMILY

The three of us were *each* trying to pull ourselves up from the dark hole of grief. Grieving is like being buried alive, requiring you to claw your way through the dirt up to the surface for air. I cannot emphasize enough the degree of incredible energy and willpower it takes to work through it. When an entire family grieves at the same time, it is difficult and sometimes lonely because the very people you would turn to for love and support are going through their own struggles. We had to respect one another as we each tried to climb back to the surface because we were digging in our own unique ways and at our own pace.

If Tom were having a day when he felt particularly strong, it would bring him down to hear me vent about how much I was struggling and missing Nick that day. Likewise, if I were having a good day, it would pull me back down by talking about Tom's pain. We wanted to support one another, but hearing about the other person's tough time just reminded us how awful things were and that the next wave of grief was just around the corner from our good day. Both of us tried our best not to drag the other one down, if we could help it.

Being parents, we always tried to make Kelli's emotions our priority regardless of what type of day we were having; however, I'm sure there were days when she was feeling better from hanging around her friends at school only to come home and find Tom and me talking about our loss or, worse yet, crying. Every day there was a different combination of who was feeling good and who wasn't. As we tried to move forward and climb out of our own holes, we were getting hit by more waves of grief striking us individually and collectively while rippling off each other with their own timing. There were a lot of moving parts.

NEW FAMILY AND NEW DYNAMIC

In a way, a child's death is the death of the entire family because the identity of that family is forever changed. I will never forget the first time Tom, Kelli, and I went out together after Nick passed. We went downtown to see *The Book of Mormon* and out to eat afterward. The whole car ride into the city was painful because half of the backseat where Nick usually sat was empty. The three of us did not talk about it, but it was the elephant in the car that was lit on fire. During that drive, it hit us that this was going to be our new family. Kelli, especially, had to feel bad because suddenly she was an only child sitting alone in the backseat. It would take time to get used to our new normal, and it was painful.

It wasn't long before we became aware that our entire family dynamic had changed. In the past, our views on many things, including Cubs vs. Sox, were often tied, two against two, with Team Kelli and Tom always up against Team Linda and Nick. Our two teams would banter and debate, which we all thoroughly enjoyed; I'm sure many families can relate. But after Nick passed, everything changed. Not only was I the only remaining Cubs fan, but I was also outnumbered in many of our new family discussions. Tom and Kelli would see things one way, and I no longer had Nick to back me up. I lost my wingman.

Kelli felt outnumbered differently. She was the only child now and suddenly had the laser-focused attention of both parents, which was a nightmare for her as it would be for any teenager. Raising a teen can be challenging for most parents, but after losing Nick, Tom and I felt we had to be especially careful with Kelli. We had just lost one kid to suicide and were shell-shocked. The thought of losing our remaining child terrified us. Kelli was at an age when most teenagers start gaining their independence, but she had two parents who wanted to Bubble Wrap and cloister her to protect her from harm and any more hurt in the world. Tom and I knew we couldn't let our fear make us overly protective because that would be unhealthy for all three of us, so we talked with one another and gave a lot of thought before making parenting decisions. We were mindful of striking a balance between protecting Kelli and letting her go out and experience the world.

Similarly, when it came to correcting Kelli, we had to figure out when it was best to cut her slack because she had been through so much, and when we had to hold firm and impose consequences for those few times she made less than stellar choices, like all teenagers do. Even though we had all been through so much, she still needed us to do our job as parents by setting boundaries and correcting her. This was challenging, especially when Tom and I did not agree on how to handle things. There were times when one of us wanted to be a little harder on Kelli and ground her, and the other felt bad for her and wanted to go easy. We just had way more to consider after losing Nick and had to work through all of it. For Tom and me, it helped to not react in the heat of the moment but instead talk through things and come up with a game plan before making significant parenting decisions. We didn't always follow this strategy and sometimes resorted to reacting on the fly, but most of the time we tried to stick to the plan.

MARRIAGE

I can understand why marriages sometimes fall apart after a loss in the family. So many things can erode the marital bond, like blame, disagreements about preceding events, differing views of an afterlife, and parenting decisions for the remaining children post-tragedy, to name a few. I cannot tell you how many times our family and friends cautioned us about taking time for each other and making sure we were kind to one another. Fortunately, Tom and I never experienced any major problems between us after Nick died. We never blamed each other for anything and continued to respect one another, even through our pain. We were in the fight of our lives, but it wasn't against each other. It was to make it through our grief.

We knew neither of us was the perfect parent, but who is? What really helped was continually keeping in mind that both of us loved Nick very much and would do anything for him. We recognized that we each missed warning signs, but they revealed themselves only with the benefit of hindsight. Neither of us had any inkling Nick was going to take his life, so we did not judge each other for missing anything. We both understood we were trying our best with what little knowledge we had at the time.

I think what also helped our marriage stay intact was our shared faith and identical views about an afterlife. We found comfort in talking about things like what we thought the other side must be like, what Nick might be doing there, and so on. Even though our good and bad days did not always coincide, we were generally moving in the same direction and progressing with our healing at about the same rate—give or take.

I'm no marriage counselor, only one person of a couple who lost their child and profoundly grieved, but if you find yourself in a similar situation and are having difficulties in your marriage, here are some things Tom and I kept in mind while we grieved that helped keep our marriage intact:

1. You and your spouse are not perfect—not perfect spouses, not perfect parents, not perfect human beings. None of us are.

2. Blaming each other is not going to bring your loved one back. He or she wouldn't want to see you and your spouse in conflict.

3. Neither of you knew what the future would bring. You both would have done anything to prevent it.

4. Hindsight is helpful, but neither of you had the benefit of it when you needed it most.

5. If you think your spouse did something wrong, consider there is a good chance your spouse is punishing himself or herself more than you know. No one goes unscathed through the grief process. We all beat ourselves up for things we said or did not say, and for things we did or did not do.

6. Your loss is challenging enough for both of you to get through. If you fight or blame each other, you are just adding to the pain of it all. You both need to forgive and let go of anger and resentment to heal.

7. If either of you did make mistakes, then learn from them. Forgive yourself and one another. Move on to live life and to love more. Do not let the tragedy of your loss compound itself and make your marriage the next casualty. Regret and remorse are two of the biggest obstacles to healing. Help one another move past them.

8. If you have other kids, remember they need you both. They just suffered a painful loss, and the last thing they need is to live with constant fighting or, worse yet, have their parents divorce.

PHYSICAL EFFECTS FROM GRIEVING

When we started grieving, Tom and I went through more physical ailments than Kelli, most likely due to our age. We were fifty-four and fifty-one, respectively. Both of us had chest pains at first and were worried one of us might even have a heart attack from grieving so hard. Tom's eye prescription was the same for over twenty years but significantly worsened in both eyes when grief struck. Fortunately, about five years later, the problem resolved itself, and the prescription changed back to what it was before the suicide. My eye prescription did not change much, but I started to see an intermittent, flashing light in the corner of one of my eyes. After seeing an eye doctor, I learned it was part of the normal aging process of the eye, but the onset happened a few weeks after Nick died, which I do not think was a mere coincidence. That flashing all but stopped a year or so later.

For a very long time, Tom and I both walked around feeling like someone had beat us up. We had aches and pains all over our bodies and were tired all the time from the stress. All three of us noticed temporary hair loss, and Tom's hair quickly turned grayer. I'm not sure if mine did because I am a woman who hasn't seen her natural color since I was about thirty-five—another Law of the Universe, although a minor one. The physical signs and effects of grieving lasted about twelve to eighteen months.

If you have recently suffered a loss, allow yourself time to work through the emotions and trials of the first year. Now more than ever, it is important to take care of yourself and your relationships. This includes being patient with yourself, your family, and your friends when the grief process turns everything on its end. It is an extraordinarily difficult time, but with love and understanding, you can help one another work through it. Life will settle down, so never lose hope. Brighter days are ahead.

Chapter 12

First Anniversary, Second Year, and Beyond

THE FIRST ANNIVERSARY

The first anniversary is tough. About a month in advance, you start feeling anxious as you count down the days until the big day. I watched the clock that first anniversary and thought about what Nick and I did the previous year for just about every hour that passed. At 9:00 a.m. I thought about how we were talking together in the hotel room, at 12:00 noon how he was probably walking toward the bridge, at 5:00 p.m. how I was talking with the detective, and so on. That was a huge mistake. I made myself miserable reliving Nick's last day. I strongly recommend that people stay away from all clocks on the anniversaries. Do something that will keep your mind engaged and make the day pass quickly, like seeing a movie, going to a play, or visiting a zoo. If you are up for it, be around family and friends who can keep you talking and distract you from reliving your painful memories.

The goal is to get through that first anniversary and honor your loved one in a way that comforts you. Be careful to not put pressure on yourself by thinking you have to do something overly creative or complex. Your goal is to just get through that first anniversary. The good news is you have completed the first, and usually the most difficult, year of grief.

THE SECOND YEAR

The second year is better than the first, although it is still very tough. You have been through everything once that comes up in a calendar year, which is a huge psychological milestone. For the most part, you are much stronger because you are able to socialize more and rebuild your life. You have good days and bad days now, whereas a year ago you had mostly bad days.

Now and then people tell me they have heard the second year is harder than the first. In my opinion, the year your loved one or friend takes his or her life, or dies in another way, is the most challenging one. The second year, however, can be grueling in its own way. It is an awakening to the harsh reality that your loss is your very own in many ways. The emptiness you feel is not going away, so you must learn to live with it and rebuild your life around that hole. At times you still struggle to get your old life back but realize you have to start over in many respects. Those people who delayed some of their grieving may be facing much of it now in the second year.

Everyone, except your immediate family, has moved on with their lives, and you start to get the feeling that a few people cannot quite understand why you have not yet recovered from your loss. I have a good friend who was amazed Tom and I had not "moved on" from losing our child after three months. Even more surprising, we have run into people who have completely forgotten what happened to us, and we have to remind them. It's rare, but it does happen.

People complain to you about their problems now, and they no longer have yours at the forefront of their minds. In a way, that is a huge compliment because they know they don't have to guard every word they speak to you, as they did throughout the past year. They feel comfortable venting to you about matters, like not being able to see their child over the holidays, while losing sight for a brief moment that you will *never* see yours again. They do things like send you a sad video clip about how time quickly passes when raising children, not thinking how time has halted for you and one of yours. Your friends, coworkers, classmates, and everyone else still very much care, but they have moved on and are no longer standing in the space beside you.

The important thing to remember is most people mean well, but you have lived through something that has ultimately changed your life forever, not theirs. It affected them, even in the most meaningful ways; nevertheless, your loss did not ultimately alter their lives, so they have naturally moved on to their own challenges. The problems they are experiencing are very real and all-encompassing to them, just like they would be for you before your loss. The more you heal, the more you will be able to relate to them. Although you have a new perspective on life challenges, with a little time, you too will start focusing on things much smaller than your loss—and that is a good thing.

In the second year, you may begin to feel uncomfortable talking about how much pain you are still experiencing because you are afraid your friends will think you cannot move on. They have patiently listened to you for a year already, so you may start worrying about becoming a drain on them. These are all very normal emotions and concerns during the second year of grieving. Hopefully, you will have some family and close friends who will be there for you when you need to talk about your grief.

Remember to seek professional help and support groups when needed.

BEYOND THE SECOND YEAR

During the second year, the permanency of your loss sinks in as you begin to build your new life. Beyond that second year, you continue to miss your loved one dearly, but you are growing generally stronger and stronger each year. Time is your friend, for sure. The anniversary of the passing and your loved one's birthday are still painful reminders of your loss, but even they get a little easier each year. Holidays, special traditions, family get-togethers, and certain celebrations continue to be challenging, but nowhere near as painful as they used to be. Each year you heal a little more because you are no longer living in grief 24/7. You miss your loved one very much and still experience pain from his or her absence; nevertheless, you know life must continue. You learn to live with your loss. I say I am now living "in loss," not "in grief."

Seven years later, I think of Nick every day and many times within a day. Tom and Kelli do pretty much the same. We have our days when we feel sad, tear up, or even cry; however, we have learned to push on. A piece of our hearts will always be missing, and things will never be the same, but we can still enjoy life. And we do. This is our new normal.

Chapter 13

A Matter of Faith

SHATTERED FAITH THEN RESTORATION AND RENEWAL

Hands down, it was my faith that got me through Nick's suicide. It was, and continues to be, an integral part of my recovery. Writing about my healing without mentioning the role faith played would be like trying to describe a Monet painting without talking about color. But first, I want to set out my intention and clarify the terminology I use.

If you have faith in a higher being, you may refer to that being as God, as I do, or as Allah, Yahweh, Jehovah, Creator, or some other name. Perhaps you identify with this supreme being as being male or female, or maybe as having no gender but consisting of pure energy of light and love. You may not believe in a higher power but place all your faith in humanity. Throughout this chapter, I refer to a higher power as God and use male pronouns, but by doing so, please know I am not trying to push my views on anyone. I have complete respect for all ideology and beliefs. Remember, this book aims to be a life preserver to help all, no matter what you believe.

I was raised Catholic. Since childhood, I would consistently go to Mass on Saturday night or Sunday but very seldom to daily Mass. I never spent a lot of time reading the Bible, other than hearing Scripture read at church each week. However, about four months before Nick passed, something strange began happening to me. Suddenly, I had a powerful urge to go to daily Mass and read the Bible, which amazed Tom as he witnessed this change unfolding.

Even my last confession before losing Nick was unusual. After telling the priest my sins, I felt the presence of God so intensely that I was moved to tears. It felt like a warm, tingling feeling all over my body but mostly in my heart. I had felt God's touch before, but not to this extent. The priest noticed my voice crack with emotion and asked if I was okay, but there was absolutely no way I was going to tell him I was crying because I was feeling God so strongly. Even to a priest, this would have sounded a bit strange, so I just said I had been going through a lot and then made light of my emotion with dry humor, like I often do. I asked him to give me a minute to collect myself before walking out of the confessional; otherwise, people in line would think I just confessed to killing someone. My humor was met with a painfully long silence.

My newfound craving for daily Mass and Scripture, as well as this experience in the confessional, made me wonder what was happening to me. In hindsight, I believe God was preparing me spiritually for the hardship that was coming around the corner.

As it turns out, all that preparation was helpful, but right after Nick's suicide, my paradigm of faith still jumbled like a Rubik's Cube that was twisted and turned out of sync. I did not lose my belief in God—thankfully that was still intact—but I could not understand how the loving God I trusted and knew so well could let such a terrible thing happen to my son.

My whole life, I tried to do everything He asked of me: I had strong faith, was loyal, and prayed to Him almost daily. Sometimes I said formal prayers like a rosary, but more often, I prayed by talking to Him casually in my head. I prayed for my kids all the time, and when it came to Nick, I was always asking God to help him and bring him friends. For the last few years of Nick's life, I repeatedly prayed for his safety and happiness.

I was certain that if you asked God for help, He would listen and answer your prayers. You may not get the result you wanted or expected every time, especially if you prayed for something that was not in alignment with His will, but you could always count on God to look out for your best interest like a parent looks after his or her child—after all, we are His children. When I prayed, I was not asking for anything like a new car or for the Cubs to win a ballgame, but rather for the happiness and safety of my child.

Long ago, I read a very popular book called *Embraced by the Light*, by Betty J. Eadie, who wrote about her near-death experience (NDE). While on the other side, God allowed Betty to see prayers from us on earth traveling to Him like beacons of light, with the most significant prayers being the brightest lights. She was told there are no greater prayers than those said by a mother for her children. They were the purest prayers because mothers made them with intense desire and sometimes out of desperation.[1]

If this is true, then God was seeing red flares from me spelling out SOS whenever I prayed for Nick, especially during his first year of college. I pleaded with Him over and over to help my son. Sometimes I even started my prayers by saying, "Hey God, SOS."

I always believed God lets us go through challenges and hardships so we can spiritually grow and advance in this world by turning to Him, relying on His help, and learning to trust Him. And that is exactly what I did. I asked God to help Nick, then relied on Him for that assistance and believed that even though Nick might be going through difficult times, God was helping him. I just assumed nothing terrible would happen to Nick . . . but he killed himself.

I wanted to know why God let that happen. Who in our family, if anyone, was meant to be challenged through Nick's struggles and eventual death? What lessons were supposed to be learned, and by whom? Nick had strong faith and was such a good person, surely something so awful as having a significant mental health crisis could not have been for *his* spiritual growth.

I also wondered why God did not put someone on the bridge to stop Nick from jumping. It was the middle of the afternoon on a weekday. Many cars were driving by, and people were all around. God easily could have had any one of them save Nick, making the final result an attempt. Then, we would have realized how much Nick needed help, allowing us the opportunity to get it for him. We absolutely would have done everything we could for Nick if we had only known the magnitude of the problem. So many other families get a warning by their loved one's attempt. Why couldn't we have had that type of heads-up? By the time I pieced together that something terrible was happening with Nick, he was already walking toward the bridge.

These were some of the questions and muddled thoughts circling in my head the first few weeks after Nick died. I was confused, hurt, and feeling something that fell in between "God let me down" and "God turned his back on me." Was I angry at God after Nick passed? You bet, but I think I was more hurt than angry. I felt like God let me down in the worst possible way, but I wasn't about to hold in any anger I did have toward Him because I knew nothing good would come from suppressing my feelings. The first chance I had to be alone, I let God have it.

Kelli was back at school, and I do not remember where Tom was other than he was not around me right then. I sat by myself in our family room, crying and trying my best to absorb that Nick was gone and never coming back. I felt God could have prevented it all. I had to try to get the feelings of disappointment and anger I had for God out of me because they were eating me up inside. I got down on my hands and knees and pounded my fists on the ground over and over and yelled, "Why didn't You help Nick? Why did You let this happen?"

I was not afraid to yell at God, not only because I felt He deserved it, but because I still knew He loved me and could take it. I lashed out holding nothing back, knowing if I didn't, I would have no chance at healing because these feelings would fester inside me and come out later in very unproductive ways. I was willing to do whatever it took to get through this pain and get better, even if it meant yelling at my Creator. I knew God and I were going to be okay in the long run, but I just needed time to work things out in my head. I was mad at Him but never lost faith that He was there the whole time holding me in the palm of His hand and loving me.

A week or so after this venting, most of the anger lifted from me, but my hurt was still there, and it was raw. Remember that jumbled Rubik's Cube of faith? Well, slowly it started to twist back into place, and I have no doubt whatsoever I was not doing any of that by myself. God was showering His healing grace upon me.

The word *grace* comes from the Greek word *charis*, which means favor, blessing, or kindness. All graces are gifts to us from God, which means we did nothing to deserve them, and nothing is owed in return. We are all born with certain graces, but God continues to give us even more as we need them. Grace is an ongoing benevolent act of God working in us and through us. He knows each of us individually, so it makes sense He would know what each of us needs in life. He gives us the proportionate amount of grace that corresponds to whatever challenge or need we face.[2]

What graces did God give me? I believe He gave me those I needed to heal, like clarity, acceptance, understanding, forgiveness, strength, fortitude, and knowledge. He gave me the **clarity** to understand the things I was supposed to know about Nick's death and to **accept** there will always be things about it that I will never comprehend in this lifetime. Through this horrible tragedy, I finally had an **understanding** on a personal level about what I had heard so many times in church—that God does not promise a happy outcome to everything in this lifetime. God never turns His back on any of us, but His ways are not our ways (Isaiah 55:8, GNT). This is something we just have to trust. This, I believe, is faith.

Through grace, I was able to **forgive** Nick for taking his life, even though I knew deep down, there was nothing to forgive. I was able to **forgive** myself, family, friends, acquaintances, and people Nick knew for whatever we all did, or did not do, that possibly contributed to Nick's pain. God gave me enough **strength** and **fortitude** so I could survive Nick's suicide and help my family heal. And if you want to look at the big picture, God even helped me heal to the extent where I could use whatever **knowledge** He gave me from my experiences with Nick, before and after his death, to help others—like writing this book.

I did nothing to deserve these graces. Nothing. And, more importantly, you do not have to do anything either, other than be open to receiving them. It does not matter who you are or what you have done in life. You were already blessed with graces at birth, and God will give you more whenever needed, provided you are open to receiving them.[3] That is how loving God is. There is absolutely no bad thing in life you could ever do that God cannot forgive. Evil wants you to believe there is, but there is not. Remember, we are all sinners and undeserving of God's graces, yet He offers them to all of us out of the pure and unconditional love He has for each one of us.

After those first few awful days of having my faith turned upside down, I realized God was carrying me in His arms and helping me restore my faith. How? He led me to go back to the basics of my faith so I could rebuild it from there. Since everything was scrambled in my head, and I didn't know what to believe anymore, I had to ask myself what I still understood to be true about God. I came up with two things: *God is good*, and *God is loving.*

This was my foundation of faith that I believed with all my heart since I was a child. I think what the Bible says is true: if you have a strong foundation of faith, you can weather the storm of anything this life throws at you—even the absolute worst. Matthew 7:24–25 says, ". . . anyone who hears these words of mine and obeys them is like a wise man who built his house on rock. The rain poured down, the rivers flooded over, and the wind blew hard against the house. But it did not fall, because it was built on rock" (GNT).[4] My foundation got shaken, for sure, but it did not crack. Even while feeling lost, hurt, and confused for some time, I never doubted God loved Nick, me, and our entire family.

Did God allow the events of Nick's death to unfold? And if so, then why would He do that—especially when Nick's decision was caused by a mental illness or condition, not free will? Even though it appeared God did not intervene, I still believed He was present and loving us through our time of need, especially Nick's. And because I knew God was good, I knew and trusted He would always look out for our best interests, even if I did not understand why bad things sometimes happen.

I kept telling myself these two principles over and over and clung to them: *God is good*, and *God is loving*. I trusted that over time, everything that confused me would eventually work itself out, and I would come to terms with not having all the answers to my questions. Everything would build and rise from the foundation of *God is good*, and *God is loving*. I knew the hurt I felt would subside over time, and God would continue to walk every step of our grief journeys with us. I never doubted the two of us would eventually be good again; we just weren't good right now.

The Sunday after I came home from Minneapolis, I went to church, but I did not want to be there and told God so. I wanted His help to heal but told Him I didn't feel like praising Him right now and was not going to fake it. I knew He was *good*, and He was *loving*, but I was still mad at Him. For the next few weeks, I did not pretend to mouth the prayers or sing in church. I couldn't even pray for Nick because that would involve praying to God, which I was not ready to do yet. I needed space and time. All the while, God kept showering me with His love and graces.

Little by little, things became clearer. I had a pretty good idea why God arranged for me to go into Jamba Juice that last day. Earlier that morning, Nick and I had a beautiful goodbye in the hotel room when he left for class. Remember, I told him, "I love you, I'm proud of you, and you are so strong." If those were my last words with Nick, I could have had some solace knowing it was a loving exchange. Instead, our final conversation ended in Jamba Juice and was somewhat chaotic.

As I looked back, it did not seem like a mere coincidence that I walked in on Nick standing at the counter. But why was I led there? I racked my brain for a week, searching for an answer. Then, a few weeks after Nick died, the reason became clearer. I may be wrong, but I think I was supposed to see the disconnect in Nick's mental functioning. Perhaps God wanted me to know that he had a mental break so I would better understand what state he was in when he ended his life. I firmly believe that when Nick jumped, he was trying to get out of pain and lift the piano off his chest. If I had never walked into that Jamba Juice, I'm sure I would have always wondered why Nick took his life when he seemed relatively upbeat as he left the hotel room that day.

Some may ask, "So if God led you to Jamba Juice, why didn't He help you stop Nick from jumping? And why didn't He put someone on the bridge to stop Nick from taking his life?" These are both fair questions; ones I asked myself over and over. My pastor recently helped me understand more about the gift of freedom that God gives creation as a whole within the boundaries of the laws of nature. He explained that if God stepped in and controlled everything in our world, then freedom would not exist. In nature, a buildup of air pressure may lead to hurricanes; falling rocks may lead to landslides; and so on. God does not predetermine those things but allows them to occur freely within the laws of nature.

Likewise, He gives all humans freedom—the freedom of choice, otherwise known as free will. He gives this gift to everyone, regardless of our mental capacity or the devastation that can result from those decisions. A mental condition (illness or disorder) may take away a person's ability to make good choices and render him or her incapable of true responsibility, but that individual still possesses the gift of free will. God does not pick and choose to whom He gives freedom, or when He will give it. Even if God disagrees with how we are about to use our gift, like when our choices will hurt ourselves or someone else, He still allows us to make those decisions and does not rescind our free will. If God intervened and controlled our choices, we would not be free.

This is not to say God does not care about the decisions we make or is hands-off. Nothing could be further from the truth. He just doesn't *force* people to act in specific ways. God will, however, try to help us along with our decisions by sending us gut feelings to act according to His will for us. Sometimes instead of gut feelings, God sends available people to our side to influence us to act in alignment with His will for us.

When Nick decided to take his life, he was exercising free will, but he did *not* have the mental capacity to be responsible for his decision. God intervened by sending Nick messages that he was loved and that he should *stay*, but due to Nick's mental illness, he could not hear God's messages. Think of Nick's mind as being like a radio that was so badly broken it was unable to tune to the "God Channel." He could not hear God telling him that He loved him and that things would get better. Nick also could not tune to the "Life Channel" and understand the messages Tom, Kelli, and I were giving him, such as things will get better and he was not a burden. His radio didn't work, and all he could hear was static, which made him dependent on others to stop him from taking his life.

I was in a turmoil that weekend trying to help Nick, which caused my radio not to have a strong connection to the God Channel, just like Nick. I was getting part of the signal, like to go to Jamba Juice where I would find Nick, but my stress and worry caused interference in receiving the part that perhaps would have warned me, through a gut feeling or something else, that Nick was about to take his life that day.

This is nothing to feel guilty about, especially because I was doing my best as a mom. At times, interference from stress and worry happens to people and is unfortunately part of life. I'm sure many parents who have helped their children through crises can relate. We are all in the trenches, putting out fires. *None of us* should feel guilty if we were doing our best but couldn't foresee our loved one's suicide. I cannot emphasize that point enough. It is pointless and unhealthy to beat ourselves up over it. God wouldn't want us to do that, and neither would our loved ones. We are human.

People around the bridge were busy doing life activities and were tuned to the Life Channel at that moment, not the God Channel. In other words, those people were also not available to gain insight from the God Channel to know Nick was about to jump. God, of course, did not want Nick to die; however, at that moment, He had no one available who could receive His message to stop Nick.

You may or may not agree with this explanation, but it has helped me, so I wanted to make it available to you. I still have many questions for God about Nick's death and believe He will answer all of them when I cross over. I don't need to know all the answers in this life and would not be able to comprehend His explanations anyhow because I can neither see nor fully understand the grand picture of God's plans for me and my loved ones. My perspective in my earthly body is limited, but I trust those plans are for our best interest. Not having answers but trusting that *God is good* and *God is loving* is faith.

I believe with all my heart that Nick is in heaven, where there is no more pain or sorrow. He is with God, who I believe is pure love. A love that we, as humans, cannot even begin to comprehend. He has a place for all of us there, no matter who we are and what we have done in our lifetimes. In my heart, again through grace, I know God heard me asking Him to help Nick, and He did so in His way. It's worth repeating: God's ways are not our ways (Isaiah 55:8). My way would have been to heal Nick and release him from the bondage of suffering that he endured here each day—to let him walk among us as a new and improved young man cured of Asperger's and of any mental illness he may have had. But God had another plan.

I know He created Nick and loved him infinitely more than I ever could because my motherly love for him was within the confines of being human. I also know God loves me, and everyone else, just as much. Therefore, my faith tells me that God heard my prayers for Nick. I think my son, and many others who struggle in this world, make an impact on people who witness their trials by bringing them to a deeper level of faith. I believe God wanted Nick to live, but when he returned home as a result of his illness, God welcomed him with open arms. Until the day I'm reunited with my son, I will trust in the goodness of God's heart and have faith in His loving actions. *God is good*, and *God is loving*—and it was God's grace that helped me understand this from the time I was a child, and to remember it after Nick died.

If you are struggling with your faith, just talk to God about it. Feel free to borrow my line: "Hey God, SOS." Be honest with Him. If you are angry with God, tell Him so. It is all right to yell at Him. Tell Him you are open to receiving His graces. Ask God to heal you, to open your heart, and to grow your faith. You are His child, and He loves you.

PRAYERFUL MOMENT IN WAITING ROOM

A month after Nick passed, I took Kelli to see a grief counselor. As I sat in the waiting room, I decided to try to pray. I didn't think I could successfully do that yet but thought I would at least go through the motions. I knew I had to get back to praying but was dragging my feet like a child. As I pulled my rosary out of my pocket, I hid it under my hand because I didn't want anyone in the waiting room to see what I was doing. As I began, I told God I was not sure I could do it. I prayed for a few minutes and then noticed a pretty Hispanic woman, who was probably in her late thirties, sitting across the room from me. She was not crying but had such a worried look on her face that it caught my attention. Every time I tried to close my eyes to pray, I found myself opening them and looking at her. She seemed almost consumed by worry.

I got up and walked over to where she was sitting and told her I just lost my son and could tell when another mom was worried about her child. Then I gave her a big hug. This could have gone south in so many different ways. She could have pulled away and looked at me like I was some weirdo, or she could have laughed at me because she was waiting not for her child, but for her husband, who was getting counseling for some foot fetish. But somehow, I knew she was sitting there waiting and worrying for her son or daughter. To my surprise, she hugged me back and asked if "the thing" I was holding in my hand was a rosary. When I said yes, she asked, "Do you know how to do that?" I told her I did and then walked back to my seat and sat down.

As I sat there, I thought, "Linda, you dummy, what are you doing? Get your butt back up and go over there and show her." In the brief time it took me to walk back, she had pulled out a rosary from her purse, along with a pamphlet in Spanish that explained how to say the rosary. She told me her mother in Mexico sent them to her. She had been carrying them around for a while but didn't know how to use them. I asked if she wanted me to show her, and with a great big smile she enthusiastically said, "Yes!" So, we sat together, and I began teaching her the basics.

We were having such a beautiful moment, just two moms sharing faith, when suddenly the door opened from the back offices, and the woman's daughter and counselor walked into the waiting area in front of us. She stood up and greeted her daughter with a smile and put her arm around her daughter's waist. The counselor wanted to talk with her, so she turned around to tell me goodbye by leaning over and giving me a big hug while thanking me for teaching her how to say the rosary.

We both seemed to know the time we just shared was very special. As my new friend left, I walked back to my seat feeling better than I had since Nick passed. While I sat there alone in the waiting room, I experienced in the quiet of my heart Mother Mary saying to me, "Just as you recognize another mother's pain, I recognize and understand yours."

SUICIDE MOM

About a month after Nick's memorial, I decided I needed to get out of our family room and start biking to get a little exercise. Near my home, a bike trail runs along the DuPage River, and it's stunningly beautiful. I had ridden the trail three or four times a week before Nick passed and was now determined to get back into a similar routine. I had gone on the trail a few times that week and was beginning a sixteen-mile bike ride on this day. It was a gorgeous June morning, the kind where the weather is so perfect you don't even notice it. The sun was brightly shining as it made its way up in a cloudless sky that was so blue it was almost periwinkle. I was looking forward to my ride because I knew the exercise would help relieve some of the stress I had been experiencing from grieving so hard. Biking was like a moving meditation that would hopefully clear my head.

Just as I started, a woman who often walked the same trail motioned for me to stop. She was attractive, very fit, and looked to be in her early sixties, with short jet-black hair cut into a pixie. For years we always smiled and said hello whenever we passed each other. There is an unspoken rule on the trail that everyone seems to obey: if you see someone walking, running, or riding their bike, you politely say hello but do not engage in idle chatter or, God forbid, real conversation. People are there for well-needed alone time to soak up the tranquility of nature and want to exercise in peace.

But that day was an exception because this woman enthusiastically gestured me to stop my bike and chat. She asked how I was doing and said she saw me yesterday morning on the trail when she was walking with two friends. I remembered passing them and made a mental note that I didn't know her companions. I acknowledged them with a quick wave and kept pedaling. She said she told her friends about me as I passed and explained to them how my son had recently "committed suicide." They talked about how hard it must have been for me. Then she looked at me with tears in her eyes and asked again how I was doing.

I could barely answer her question. First of all, the phrase she used—"committed suicide"—just hung in the air. I had heard it many times before, and even used it myself, but never realized how it makes a person sound. Criminals *commit* crimes and cheaters *commit* adultery. Nick *died* by suicide: he did not *commit* it. He was not a criminal or an adulterer. Of course, I knew she didn't mean it that way, but the phrase still stung. Second, two women I had never met and another woman I barely knew all had a conversation about Nick's darkest moment and my deepest pain. Part of me appreciated their concern for me and felt guilty thinking anything negative about it. These people were probably being compassionate, not gossiping; however, it had only been a month since Nick died. The topic was still so raw and personal, and I couldn't help but be bothered by these strangers freely discussing it. How did they even find out that he took his life? I only knew this lady well enough to wave to her on the trail.

Word of Nick's suicide was apparently spreading quickly around town. How could they possibly know what Nick was going through? They never even met him. Did they feel sorry for him, or did they just assume his suicide was a result of some awful teenage angst? They didn't know me either, so were they empathic or were they critical of me? I wondered if they judged that my husband and I somehow lowered Nick's self-esteem or put too much pressure on him. Then, right at that moment, it hit me . . . I was forever going to be known as "Suicide Mom."

I lived my whole life staying within the lines, never really wanting to draw attention to myself. I genuinely cared about what people thought and wanted everyone to think well of me. I always tried to do the right thing and was such a goody-goody my whole life; it was almost sickening. When I was younger, I was an honor student, a cheerleader, and a musician. I was a polite people-pleaser. In my twenties and early thirties, before I had kids, I worked hard at being a conscientious lawyer and a good wife. I followed everyone's rules and never even got a speeding ticket. If anything in my life remotely looked like it wouldn't work out well, I just worked harder and did whatever it took to wrangle a more favorable outcome.

I quit my full-time law job when I was pregnant with Nick and stopped practicing law entirely when Kelli was born so I could stay at home with both kids. I took them to all kinds of park district classes and other extracurricular activities, chaperoned many school field trips, and drove them to school each day.

I volunteered to be room mom, an art awareness mom, and a member of the grade school and middle school hospitality committees. Through our church, I taught my kids' religion classes from kindergarten through fifth grade and even continued teaching other children after Nick and Kelli were in middle school. My world revolved around my kids. I'm pretty sure I had the reputation of being a good mom who would do anything for her children.

I mention my past deeds not to be obnoxious but to explain how all my previous efforts, dedication to my kids, accomplishments, and good reputation did not seem to matter now. It felt like Nick's suicide erased it all and branded me not as a good mom but as the mom whose kid jumped off a bridge—and there was not a darn thing I could do about it. Like everyone else, I shuddered at the thought of people taking their lives and using the "s" word. But at that moment, I knew I would forever be linked to suicide.

So as the woman asked how I was doing, I became flustered and was barely able to answer her. I told her I was okay and briefly explained how it was difficult, but I was getting through it. I thanked her for caring, then got back on my bike and rode away as fast as I could because I knew I was going to break down and cry. As I rode alongside the river, I looked toward the sky and its rising sun with tears in my eyes. I let out a big sigh in defeat and under my breath said to God, "I'm forever going to be known as Suicide Mom."

Suddenly, an eerily peaceful feeling came over me. Inside my heart, I felt God was telling me this was the role he wanted for me and was asking me to fulfill. He was saying, "Yes, will you do that for Me?" God was asking if I would be the face and voice for suicide because maybe when people see me, they will go home and hug their children. Perhaps they will remember how important it is to give their kids all the care they need and to seek professional help when necessary. At that moment, I had a pretty good idea of the magnitude and breadth of what He was asking—the pain, the sacrifice, the dedication. "Yes, I will be your Suicide Mom," I answered quietly from my heart as I hung my head and continued riding.

If you find yourself being Suicide Mom, Suicide Dad, Suicide Sibling, or Suicide Friend, join me in saying yes to using the experiences of our loved ones to help others. No doubt, it calls for a life of sacrifice and challenge, but we can make a difference. We may not have been able to save our loved ones, but we can use what we learned to try to help others. Through our pain, we have learned much. I believe this is what our loved ones would want, and I have no doubts that they will assist us along the way.

FORGIVENESS

Years ago, when my kids were toddlers playing in our family room, I would sometimes turn on *Oprah*. This was back in the 1990s when her show was still on network television. As a stay-at-home mom, there were days when this was my only contact with adults and the outside world. I'm sure many stay-at-home parents can relate. Every now and then Oprah would have a show featuring parents whose child had been molested or murdered, and she would ask them how they were coping with such a horrific loss. Their responses always amazed me because they all said, in one way or another, that to move on with their lives it was necessary to forgive the person who hurt their child.

I wondered how in the world they had the strength and compassion to do this. Sure, many people can forgive others when they have disagreements or arguments. They can even do so when they have been lied to or cheated on by someone they trusted; however, to forgive the person who badly hurt or killed your child is a whole different category of forgiveness—one that seemed almost impossible to me.

When the time came for Tom, Kelli, and me to forgive the people who hurt Nick, we were surprised that it took less effort than we expected. Now granted, Nick was not molested or murdered, but throughout his entire life, people did very unkind things to him, which, in my opinion, significantly contributed to his death—yet it was still possible to forgive them.

A week after Nick died, Tom drove back to the University of Minnesota to clean out his dorm room. My dear cousin Bill and our close friend Faruk accompanied him, knowing how difficult this would be for him. Nick's roommate was sitting at his desk when Tom walked into the room. Tom asked him for some privacy while he packed Nick's belongings. As the roommate stood up to leave, Tom told him Nick had the best heart of anyone he had ever known, and with that, the roommate's eyes welled up with tears as he looked down toward the floor. Seeing how emotional the boy was, Tom walked over, hugged him, and said, "I don't know what happened here between Nick and all you guys on the floor, but there has been enough tragedy." Then he reminded the roommate that words have consequences and told him that they all should be kind to everyone, especially others not like themselves. I believe the forgiveness Tom showed that day could be done only with God's grace.

At birth we are all given the grace we need to forgive; moreover, when exceptional circumstances arise that call for an almost superhuman kind of forgiveness, we are given additional grace to forgive in that capacity as well. In fact, grace is precisely that— super(above)human. It comes from God. It allows us to do, through God, what we never thought would be possible, and would be impossible, without Him.[5]

As a young mom in my family room, I could not understand how those *Oprah* parents could forgive the people who hurt their children because I never needed to forgive people in that way—or on that level. No one had ever caused or contributed to the bodily harm of my kids. After Nick died, however, God gave the three of us the proportionate amount of grace needed to forgive within our extraordinary circumstances—just like He gave to those parents. Much later, I finally understood how we could forgive like that: we were not doing it on our own. I have no idea whether it was a special type of grace God gave us or just more of what we already had from birth, but what I do know is that Tom, Kelli, and I now possessed an ability to forgive on a level and in a way that we could not do in the past.

The three of us are ordinary people. We are sinners like everyone else, but we wanted to forgive the people who hurt Nick and were open to receiving God's grace to do that. We also forgave, in part, so that we could heal. To me, forgiveness is when you wish people well in life, even though they hurt you or your loved ones. You may still feel some pain when you think about what harm they caused, and you remember what they did or failed to do, but you do not dwell on it. Deep in your heart, you wish them well. You move on. We had to let go of the fact that certain people caused Nick and our family pain because if we didn't, it would have taken us down and made us bitter. We had to forgive them because we wanted to heal, and we knew it was the right thing to do. Now when I say The Lord's Prayer (The Our Father) and come to the part that says, "Forgive us our trespasses as we forgive those who trespass against us," I think of all those people who hurt Nick and our family. They are a reminder that just as God helped me to forgive them, He has also forgiven me for all my sins.

God's graces are for everyone because He loves us all. Know that you always have the ability to forgive under any circumstance and in every situation. If ever there comes a time you need the type of grace our family needed, or any other kind, trust God is there for you and is giving you what you need. God provides each of us with *precisely* the grace we need when we *need* it. Just be open to receiving His help. How does God know if you are open to receiving it? He's God. He knows your heart.

If you ever find yourself having a difficult time forgiving someone, trust that God has given you the ability to do so and is waiting by your side until you are open to receiving His help to forgive. Just try your best and keep praying for God to help you find the desire to forgive. Trust God will do His part. When your heart warms, cooperate, and try your best to offer that forgiveness.

Perhaps you think you did something terrible in life, and God does not want to help you anymore. Nothing could be further from the truth. We all stumble and fall. It does not matter what you have done in your past. If you want God's forgiveness, He gives it to you. If you want His help, He gives it to you—period. Ask Him for the grace to first forgive yourself for whatever you have done, and then to help you forgive the people you want to forgive. He loves each and every one of us, no matter what we have done or what we do.

What if you don't want to forgive someone? I encourage you to keep praying and ask God to help soften your heart for that person. I hope you try to forgive, though, because if I had not done so, I know I never would have been able to heal from Nick's suicide as much as I have. None of my family could have. We would all be bitter and angry . . . and that is no way to live.

Chapter 14

Choices, Changes, and Self-Growth

After losing Nick, I faced a lot of choices and changes in my life. I had to decide whether to see myself as a victim and view Nick's suicide as something done to me—or to look at Nick's death as a tragedy that I could, and would, survive. In other words, I had to choose whether I was going to give up or work through the grief and loss. Then, once I decided to do the work, I had to decide how I was going to do it. Would it be best to lay low and continue the activities I had been doing before Nick's death? Or should I put myself out in the world and use his suicide to help others?

Simultaneously, I found myself gradually growing and changing because I was gaining new perspectives on topics such as when I have control in life, how I viewed life and death, what things I considered to be important, and how I should parent going forward.

New choices and changes are inevitable after a significant loss, a tragedy, or both because your old life no longer exists. You are no longer the person you used to be. It is up to you to decide how you want to proceed. Do you give up, coast, or dig in and rebuild your life? What if you don't want to give up but have absolutely no idea what to do? Well, this is understandable because your world has just flipped upside down. You may no longer be sure what you are capable of doing. Try not to worry because having these questions and doubts is very normal. I had them too. I am sharing my thoughts and feelings to help comfort you in knowing you are not alone in doubting yourself when trying to figure out your next step. Hopefully, my journey will provide some takeaways that will give you the confidence to forge your path. Remember, many roads lead to a happy future.

CHOICES AFTER A TRAGEDY, A SIGNIFICANT LOSS, OR BOTH

I believe there are four basic categories of choices people make when they experience a tragedy (including traumatic events), a significant loss, or both. I must, however, digress before I explain these choices to point out why I distinguish tragedy from significant loss when describing these choices. Every tragedy involves a significant loss of someone or something, but not all significant losses are tragedies. If your friend or loved one died by suicide, you would undoubtedly consider it a tragic event *and* a significant loss, right? However, if your ninety-five-year-old mother passed away in her sleep, most would consider that a significant loss but not a tragic event. Likewise, I viewed my parents' divorce to be a significant loss, not a tragedy (although, certainly some divorces can be very traumatic).

It may seem rigid to name categories when talking about life choices; however, when people go through these emotional experiences, often everything becomes blurred. Giving a little structure to that blur can be very helpful. The four basic categories of choices are:

1. Allow tragedy/loss to compound itself and destroy the quality of life.

2. Allow tragedy/loss to take away all hope or ambition for a good future and survive by doing nothing more than "getting by" in life.

3. Accept tragedy/loss, try best to heal, and move on by living productively in ways that have nothing to do with the topic of the tragedy/loss, such as taking classes, doing volunteer work (again, outside the scope of tragedy/loss), continuing in a job, and/or caring for a family.

4. Accept tragedy/loss, try best to heal, and use the same tragedy/loss to help others who suffer under similar circumstances, or have the potential to do so.

An example of parents who chose pathway three made the news a few years ago. That mom and dad suffered an unimaginable loss and tragedy at Disney World when an alligator snatched their two-year-old boy right in front of them and dragged him into a lagoon. The gator eventually released their son, but he died from drowning. Soon after, the parents established a foundation that raises funds for families of children receiving organ transplants in the Omaha, Nebraska, area.[1]

These parents chose to see themselves as survivors, not victims, who could do much good in life. Their charitable work is somewhat outside the scope of their traumatic event (although they are helping families fighting for their children's lives—as they did). It is an incredible nonprofit organization. Even if they had not formed a charity but still chose to live a good, productive life in other ways, they would fall under category three.

So how did I choose my path after Nick's death? I knew I was a fairly strong person because I had made it through some pretty tough life challenges, like my parents' divorce and some serious health issues within our family. And even though losing a child is so much more difficult than anything I had experienced, I still figured I was strong enough not to view myself as a victim. All this gave me the confidence to know I probably would not fall into category one or two and could work through my grief to the point of volunteering within my community, as I did before Nick passed. I just did not want the work to have anything to do with mental health issues or suicide. Who could blame me for trying to avoid reliving my son's death over and over?

My initial plan was to rebuild my life in a way that would fall within category three, but the world had different plans for me. Ultimately, I wound up living life and doing the work that falls under category four. Pathways three and four can be equally productive and satisfying—not just for me, but for everyone.

As early as four weeks after Nick's passing, I felt like I was being "called" to go down the path of option four, not three, and help others by using Nick's story. I had absolutely no idea how I was supposed to do that, though. Shortly after Nick passed, Tom and I formed a not-for-profit charity called Nick's Network of Hope. I knew I could do suicide prevention work under that name and could also help suicide loss survivors if I decided to do that later.

Once I formed the nonprofit, part of me still tried to talk myself out of working in areas involving suicide. I battled with this internal conflict on and off for about three years. I was all right with being Suicide Mom but didn't want to work in that role every day. Many questions circled in my head. Did I really want to do something that would continuously remind me of Nick's painful life and death? What was I specifically meant to do? And did I have the skills it would require? I mulled over all this while trying to heal from losing Nick, and it became overwhelming.

Something like an invisible force was pulling me toward doing suicide prevention work but not defining what I was supposed to do. I eventually came to realize I could not try to see the big picture all at once. It was way too big. I carved out time and sat in silence each day to try to figure things out, trusting that when the timing was right, I would get more direction.

In the meantime, I kept thinking back to Nick alone in his room searching the internet for answers to his questions about his mental health, and I knew there were many more people in the world doing the same. I also imagined flustered, hurried, and stressed-out parents going on their computers looking for information that could help them care for their children. All this weighed heavily on me. After three years of constant thought, and with all those people in mind, I created the website nicksnetworkofhope.org. Nicksnetworkofhope.org is an information portal with all kinds of useful information and links for many life challenges: depression, suicide, eating disorders, LGBTQ, cutting, self-harm, anxiety, substance abuse, and addiction. Since launching it, I've added valuable resources to help people make it through grief and loss.

I didn't know the first thing about how to put a website together and was not computer savvy at all; however, after a pretty laborious summer teaching myself, I created a comprehensive website. Do not be afraid to reach beyond what you think you can achieve as you build your life again. You will be amazed at what you can accomplish.

I began to do suicide prevention work within my community, but the whole time I felt this yearning, pulling, calling, or whatever you want to call it, to write this book and do public speaking. This feeling would not leave me alone, no matter how much I tried to dismiss it—and believe me, I tried.

Now I would love to say that by this point, I was entirely on board with whatever I was meant to do, but I was *still* resisting a little. I worried that writing and giving talks about Nick's suicide would be too emotionally draining and set me back in my healing. I wondered if I had the skills to write a book or do public speaking, and the thought of both frightened me. It took some time, but I had to learn to trust that if I leaped out of my comfort zone, I could accomplish more than I ever thought possible. What I didn't know how to do, I would figure out. I could not waste my energy worrying about what I was going to do, or if I possessed the ability to do it. All I had to do was say yes to the work and have faith the resources, information, and messages would go to the right people, at the right time, and help those in need. It was never about me in the first place; it was *always* about the people and the work.

If you find yourself healing from a traumatic event, like the loss of a loved one, I encourage you to believe in yourself and trust that you can pull yourself out of your grief to live a very productive life, not merely get by. As long as you keep moving forward (categories three and four), you can do any number of things with your life and be happy. Remember, you do not have to decide any of it right away. In fact, you should not jump into something during that first year when you are heavily mourning. Take one step at a time and heal (give yourself time, go to a grief counselor, and/or attend a support group), discern (sit in quiet and reflect), and then act. If you try to see the big picture of what you will do for the rest of your life and want all the answers upfront, you may feel overwhelmed and get numbed by fear.

Keep in mind that you are much stronger than you think and can do more than you ever dreamed possible. You don't have to do something big; do small things with love and kindness. Your tragedy or loss has most likely given you more empathy and compassion for others in pain. This insight will transcend into all areas of your life. You have a purpose in life and are meant to do more than merely react to your hardship. Live your life and become your best self.

OPPORTUNITY FOR SELF-GROWTH

Change in Self-Image

There's nothing quite like a life-altering event to open your eyes and make you re-evaluate . . . well, pretty much everything. If you are stuck in your views before it happens, the jolt blows everything wide open. You suddenly get an up-close look at who you really are and what perspectives you have in life. It can be very enlightening. The hardship causes you to turn inward and reflect on who you want to be in the future, as well as what you hold important and want to value moving forward. I think this happens because life as you once knew it has been shattered, and you are left to pick up the pieces, deciding what goes back together and what needs to be discarded or changed.

The only people who don't do this type of work are the ones who take on a victim mentality. People who see themselves as victims do not look inward at themselves or their lives, nor do they see much of a future. Their old lives are gone, and they refuse even to try to recreate new ones. Instead, they spend their time blaming others or things for ruining their lives. They cannot get past thoughts like, "What did I ever do to deserve this? Why me? Why does the world have it out for me?"

It is typical to have some of these thoughts right after a tragedy or loss, but if you are still doing it months later, then perhaps your attitude is getting in the way of healing. If you think the world is against you and somehow owes you, or that life is terrible and will never get better, then you see yourself as a victim. Another hazard of the victim mentality is that you may begin seeing yourself as weak and unable to control your destiny. You may believe you are incapable of rebuilding your life. And once you stop trying to heal, you run the risk of becoming bitter and miserable.

You may never move forward if you only see yourself as a victim. If, however, you can view your tragedy or loss as something that happened and hurt you but did not destroy you, and if you value life as still worth living, then you can open yourself to finding hope and seeing the good in the world again. Hopefully, you will eventually realize that the hardship you endured, though painful and even devastating, has made you stronger in some way. Take the opportunity to make some positive changes in your life as you rebuild and move on.

Tom, Kelli, and I do not consider ourselves victims: we are survivors. At first, we wondered, "Why us?" Why did something so awful have to happen to us? Thankfully, we eventually moved past that point. Life can be heartbreaking at times, but we still view it as a beautiful gift. All three of us believe that as long as we are alive, we still have our missions to fulfill and much to contribute to this world. Every day we have the opportunity to do something good for someone. If we can survive losing Nick, we can get through anything. Any other challenges, like minor medical issues, job changes, and relationship conflicts, seem small and very manageable compared to what we've already experienced. Although we will always feel some pain from our loss, we are still strong.

Long ago, Tom told me a story about a man who suffered a lot in his life but came through it with an inner strength that could never be broken. He was an elderly Jewish gentleman who owned some commercial real estate with a loan that was in default. Tom, acting on behalf of his employer, had to foreclose on his property, and the man decided to settle the foreclosure lawsuit by forfeiting the title to his property.

When the gentleman was packed up and ready to leave the premises, he thanked Tom and told him he had to deal with many businesspeople over the years, but no one treated him with the kindness and respect Tom had shown him throughout the process. Even though he lost his property, he knew it wasn't the end of the world. This man had no doubts he would be okay because he had suffered so much worse in his life. He knew his strength and understood he was not a victim. He was a survivor—a lesson he learned while suffering in the concentration camps of the Holocaust.

Change in Priorities and Perspectives

Weathering the storm of Nick's suicide not only allowed me to figure out who I was and what I was made of but also provided me the opportunity to slow down and examine my priorities and perspectives. I always tried to put God first and my family second, which are good priorities, but Nick's suicide made me reconsider what else I thought was important in life.

What's Important in Parenting

While raising my kids, I spent much time organizing and cleaning; creating family schedules; researching academic, extracurricular, and social opportunities for my kids; and driving them to all their activities. When they were in grade school, I figured out which classes and programs they needed to prepare for their middle school years, and when they were in middle school, I researched what was required to excel in high school, and so on. You get the idea—I was a type A mom always looking ahead and strategizing.

By the time my kids got into high school, they shared in the task of finding their activities and programs and willingly overbooked themselves with hard courses, extracurricular activities, and volunteer work because most kids in our area were doing the same. Some of the volunteering they wanted to do, but to be honest, not all of it. Nick and Kelli did it anyway because they felt they had to grab whatever opportunities they could to put on their college applications. Both went to tutors, too. Nick and Kelli had little downtime, just like every other kid, and it sickened me. Yet like most parents in my community, I felt pressure to make sure my kids were doing all the right things to "get ahead in life."

Nick didn't do many sports, but Kelli did. She had fun doing them, but like many kids, she stayed on at least one team longer than she wanted because it would balance out her activities when she applied to college. Does any of this sound familiar? Many kids at the area high schools were doing sports to try to get accepted to particular colleges or to get awarded scholarships. Overall, the time commitment of middle school and high school sports was sometimes brutal on these kids.

Nick and Kelli knew Tom and I always wanted them to try their best at everything they took on. They didn't have to *be* the best; we just hoped they would be their own *personal* best by giving their all to anything they took on. We told them repeatedly that we would be okay with whatever grades they came home with, and with whatever outcomes happened, as long as they were putting forth their full effort. I know they not only heard our message but understood it as well. We thought we were good parents by telling them this, but in hindsight, it was not enough.

The fact is, Nick, Kelli, Tom, and I were all victims of the treadmill that many people are on today to prepare our youth for their future. In hindsight it was, and still is, eating up our kids and spitting them out. I wish we would have had the foresight and courage to jump off that treadmill long ago. Life is too short and precious to overbook and schedule every moment, especially at such a young age.

I look back and realize we wasted precious time together, chasing after accomplishments that were somewhat unrealistic and too demanding for kids. I wish I would have told them to take whatever courses they wanted, within reason, not always the ones they felt they needed to have on their college applications. The same goes for extracurricular activities. If I could do it all over again, I would encourage them to do only the extracurriculars that really interested them and made them happy, and not worry so intensely about their college applications or job resumes. I would also tell them to have more fun and make sure to take some time to relax and enjoy their youth.

When I was a kid, we did about an hour of homework then ran out of the house to ride bikes, play ball, or catch caterpillars in an empty coffee can. Even in high school, most of us didn't stay up late doing homework each night. Now kids stay after school for several hours doing coordinated, scheduled extracurricular activities; come home and grab a quick bite to eat; and then do homework until very late at night. Many even stay up to the early hours of the morning to fit in everything they have to do. Our young people are walking around stressed and sleep-deprived day after day. Even though these kids may want to, they cannot stop this craziness because they believe they have to keep up with their peers, who are also overscheduled. Instead of jumping off the treadmill, too many of them are jumping off bridges and buildings, or chairs with nooses around their necks.

The kids who plan to go to college feel the pressure to make good grades and be involved in a multitude of activities in the hope of making their college applications competitive. The students who are not planning to attend college often feel the academic pressures as well. They need to learn a vocation, which frequently involves balancing part-time work, extracurricular experiences, and schooling. These kids have to be competitive in the job market to find a good-paying full-time job with decent benefits once they leave school.

With the help and sometimes even acquiescence of parents and other adults, kids are overscheduling themselves and enduring stress that is proving over time to be breaking them. If you doubt this, look to our increasing suicide rates. According to the Centers for Disease Control and Prevention (the CDC), suicide is the second leading cause of death for people between the ages of ten and thirty-four.[2]

Losing my son jolted me to take a closer look at society and re-evaluate what is important. It gave me a whole new perspective on parenting. It suddenly became clear to me that everything we are all doing while on that treadmill is not nearly as crucial as I once thought. The pressure we put on our kids about extracurricular activities, the countless hours of homework, and the over-the-top job and college searches no longer seemed as important. Likewise, the pressure we put on ourselves as parents—like being master researchers, organizers, and schedulers for our kids and their activities—no longer seemed as important. The need to have everything in our lives always in order no longer seemed important. None of it seemed as important anymore as the health and well-being of ourselves and our children.

It doesn't matter if your house is clean and you are well organized if your child is sitting in a spotless bedroom feeling like he cannot go on. Your daughter probably doesn't care what college preparatory program she is in if she doesn't have time for friends or hope for a future. It doesn't matter what college your son got accepted to if he is planning on taking his life there. If your daughter dies by suicide, it doesn't matter if she was an honor student, in AP classes, or on the varsity team. And it doesn't matter what job your son got if he won't be alive much longer to work there.

If all that is not important, what is? After Nick died, I spoke with my friend Fran, a nurse who works at a behavioral and mental health center in our area. She believes, like many mental health professionals, that one of the primary factors hurting our youth, besides overscheduling, is their lack of coping skills to handle stress. I spent a lot of time thinking about that and decided she is absolutely right. I now understand that the most important thing—and where our main focus needs to be—is not on which academic or extracurricular programs our children are in but rather how well they are prepared to handle life in general.

We should be asking ourselves things like, "Do my kids love themselves? Do they love others? Can they forgive themselves and others? Are they kind, compassionate, and empathetic? Do my kids have what it takes to pick themselves up after disappointments and failures? Are they good at problem-solving? Do they have a positive outlook on life?" If the answer is yes to these types of questions, then chances are they will be successful in life no matter what job they get or what college they attend. *These* are the lessons that parents, teachers, coaches, and anybody else who interacts with kids should be teaching our youth. *These* are the things that matter and will help save our kids from falling into depression and dying from suicide.

In addition to teaching these lessons, we should let kids do more things on their own. I looked back at my parenting and what came to mind was that, like many parents, I always tried to help my kids avoid making mistakes because I wanted to save them from as many negative experiences as possible. Hey, we all want to see our kids succeed and be happy, right? But as I reviewed my parenting, I could not help but wonder if I, like many parents in my generation, did a little too much for my kids.

We can't be afraid to let our kids go through disappointments, make mistakes, and experience minor failures now and then because they can learn from them. They need to see for themselves that sometimes even when they are trying their best, things don't work out as planned. It's disappointing, but it is not the end of the world. They will survive. If they make mistakes or bad choices, they need to be able to forgive themselves, learn their lessons, and move on. They must learn to cope with failure and disappointment because life lessons and challenges are going to come their way at some point, and they must be equipped to handle them.

If we do not allow them to learn how to cope, we are setting them up for a lifetime of pain and suffering. They will endure stress when things do not go perfectly and not be resilient enough to problem solve. Even when they can, they may lack the confidence to try to work things out. They may have difficulties finding hope in challenging situations. Letting them experience their minor failures also allows them to gain self-esteem and a real sense of pride in their accomplishments when they do succeed.

I think many parents in my generation, Tom and I included, bent over backward to keep their kids from failing or experiencing disappointment. We helped our kids with their projects or even did the work for them. We drove them back to school whenever they forgot their books or gym shorts, corrected their homework before they turned it in, micromanaged everything they did, and scheduled all their activities. Our parents' generation never did that for us.

As kids, my generation used to take off after school and, except for the dinner hour, never saw our parents until bedtime. If we didn't understand our homework, it was up to us to stay after school and ask for help. And if we didn't, we stayed confused. If we wanted to make the team, we had to figure out what was required, and then it was up to us to do it. If we didn't follow up with what we needed to do, we suffered the outcome. We missed opportunities and failed at things, but we still lived. These lessons taught us our efforts paid off. Our actions, and sometimes inactions, had consequences. If we made mistakes, we had to take responsibility for them, and then our parents made us fix the problems. If life didn't go our way, and we complained about it to our parents, they told us to toughen up.

Okay, most people my age can agree that sometimes our parents were a little extreme at times, but they got some of it really right. I wish I had been a bit more like that generation and let my kids learn for themselves how to fail, provided they were not in harm's way, of course. When we do too much for our kids, like coordinating all their activities, helping them with all their homework, and not allowing them to experience minor failures, we inadvertently send them the message that we think they cannot do these things on their own and succeed.

Nick probably had one or more mental health issues, so in hindsight doing more for him and protecting him from failure may have been the right thing to do—or perhaps it put additional pressure on him. I will never know for sure. However, after losing Nick, I asked myself how I wanted to change when parenting

Kelli. After some discernment, I decided it would be best to let her do more for herself, which included making mistakes. So, after making sure Kelli was safe and healing well, I lovingly pulled back and oversaw her as she did more of her own thing while away at college—and still do now.

At first, it was tough to let go because I wanted to protect her, especially after everything she had gone through, but I knew it was the right thing to do. I was there for her whenever she needed me, but I was not going to do as many things for her as I had in the past. If I thought she had any mental health issue, I, of course, would never have pulled back so much. The truth is, she was old enough that she probably would not have listened to me telling her what to do or let me do too many things for her anyhow. And that type of independence is a good thing.

When kids learn how to solve their problems, and their accomplishments become their own, they become more resilient and much happier people with more self-esteem. Even when they fail and make mistakes, kids learn their lessons and figure out how to bounce back. They become hopeful that their run at the next challenge will be better. I am grateful to gain these perspectives and understandings, and I'm not sure I would have this insight to the extent I do if I did not go through something as traumatic as losing a child.

Control

What is that saying . . . if you want to make God laugh, tell him your plans? I used to think I could control most things if I worked hard enough. Nick's death made me understand I cannot. Suddenly, it became clear that many things I used to worry about were out of my control, so it was pointless to stress over them. After we do our best with something, why don't we just let it go and have faith that life will bring us the outcome we need to learn and grow from that experience? We have a finite amount of energy to use each day, and we need to choose wisely how we expend it. Having gone through something that was out of my control and as awful as losing a child, I learned to spend way less time trying to plan, schedule, and organize because I realized I could not and cannot control my future that way, nor guarantee my happiness.

Look closely at your life. What are you doing unnecessarily in an attempt to have control? Now I live more in the moment, which gives me more time to enjoy myself and my relationships. I am by no means saying it is not worth attempting to have a good handle on things or that organization is not good, but rather, when your efforts reach a point where you are rigidly controlling people or matters, then you may need to ask yourself what's your motivation. I accept that I am not in control, and sometimes I will face an unexpected outcome—and that's okay. Trying to control everything is not only impossible but also exhausting because when things do not go as you planned, you feel personally responsible for letting people down. Gaining this new perspective about control was liberating.

Life and Death

Suffering a significant loss may also change your perspective on life and death. My mother passed the year after Nick died. She was diagnosed with stage four lung cancer and died seven weeks later. Nothing could be done for her medically, and she was in hospice for her remaining seven weeks in our home. It was my honor and blessing to care for her until the end. My aunt, who was like a second mother to me, passed away after Nick but before my mother. That was a whole lot of loss in just over a year and a half, and of family members I loved dearly. I was surprised I didn't go into some depression or funk afterward, but I think the experience of losing a child somehow changed me and gave me a new perspective on life and death—and my mom's and aunt's deaths reinforced that new perspective.

Nick's passing opened my eyes to see life as more meaningful and fleeting. We are in this world to love one another, positively affect each other, and learn our lessons. When my mom and aunt passed, instead of focusing on their deaths, I could now look more thoroughly at how we spent our time together while they were alive. I thought about what I learned from them in the short time they were here and was thankful for the time we shared. I celebrated the love between us. My loved ones died, but my past relationships with them and the love we shared did not. Now granted, I could not do all this right away after Nick's suicide because he was my child, and he died so young and tragically. However, it was his death that helped me gain this new perspective and made it possible to keep my head on straight when confronted with the loss of my aunt and mother so soon afterward.

Suffering a significant loss, tragedy, or both can provide an opportunity for personal growth with changes in priorities and perspectives. It allows you to slow down and take a look at how you want to move forward with your life. Then once you are ready, you can use all the ways you have grown from your experience to move ahead with confidence.

Chapter 15

Practical Tips for Loss Survivors

I have been a suicide loss survivor for seven years now. When I became a member of this group, I wanted to talk with someone who had gone through the same loss. I desperately needed answers to my questions: How healed would I be in one year? Five years? Ten years? What must I do to give myself the best shot at having a somewhat normal life again?

I don't know where I will be in ten years, but I can share what helped me get to the seven-year mark in pretty decent shape. I don't claim to have the secret decoder ring for all the trials suicide loss survivors face; furthermore, what works for me may not work for you because everyone heals differently, but I will gladly share what helped my family and me. But first, if you are having a difficult time even starting to heal or feel like you are stuck in your grief, here are some practical reminders from the mother in me about why you should keep pushing on after your loss:

REASONS TO KEEP PUSHING ON

❊ **You deserve to enjoy life.** We all do. Our loved ones would want us to continue to do good things in life and enjoy ourselves.

❊ **You are valuable.** Your family needs you. The world needs you. I believe we are meant to reach out and lovingly serve one another. You have gone through something that, hopefully, has given you more empathy and understanding for others who may be struggling. Once you heal and feel strong, you may choose to use your experience to help others. Even in your day-to-day relationships, your newfound perspective and compassion has the potential to comfort others and deepen your relationships, all while bringing you joy.

❊ **Your life is worth living.** What are you going to do, just lay there in the fetal position and give up? You may feel like that for the first few months of grieving, but you have to pick yourself up off the floor. Are you going to numb yourself with drugs or alcohol? The sooner you face your loss, the quicker you will begin the healing process. It is arduous work but worth the effort. Many support groups and professionals can help you, so do not feel like you must go through it alone. Life is still good and very much worth living even after a loss.

❊ **You don't want to make the tragedy worse.** If you choose not to live your best life possible or give up and stop engaging with others, then the tragedy of your loss has extended to you. Instead of one life lost, now there are two.

❊ **You may be a role model.** If you have kids or other family members who look to you for guidance, consider that how you handle your loss may influence how they cope with their disappointments and loss—now and in the future.

RECOMMENDATIONS
(WHAT WORKED FOR US)

Rely on Your Faith

My faith got me through Nick's suicide. I covered this at length in chapter 13, but it's worth briefly mentioning again. I relied heavily on my faith; it was my primary source for healing. If you have faith, hold it close and trust that you can weather any storm. If you think you lack faith, ask God for help because it is a gift He freely gives.

If you do not believe in a higher power but place all your faith in humanity or something else entirely, then rely on certain people or that other source to help you get through your grief.

Train Your Brain

Tom and I began to realize that a big part of our healing was training our brains to shift or divert specific thoughts. Let me explain. In the first stages of grief, we thought of the worst moments of our loss over and over. We did not set out to do this; it just naturally happened. We thought about the details of Nick's mental illness and death forward, backward, and sideways. We thought of him as being sad, weak, confused, and distracted. We tried to imagine his pain, his last thoughts, and even the moment of his death. These thoughts circled through our heads again and again. It was excruciating. I believe this type of thinking is fairly typical for most people after they lose someone.

Eventually, we got sick and tired of those dark and gloomy images and memories. We wore out those thought patterns in our brains. I think it is not only healthy but necessary to allow yourself to circle in the ugliness until you get a bellyful. Why? Because you are allowing yourself time to process the darker parts of the tragedy. But to continue to heal, you eventually have to get out of that mindset and set that darkness free. You must work at bringing lighter and brighter thoughts into your mind.

When we reached that point in healing where we grew sick and exhausted from thinking about Nick's death, and all the moments leading up to it, then we believed we were ready for a change. Whenever the negative thoughts popped into our heads, we worked on quickly shifting them to more positive and grateful ones. If you are a person of faith or spirituality, you may start thinking of your loved one as they are now in the afterlife—on the other side feeling healthy and strong—rather than thinking of them as how they were here—ill and in pain, for example. And whether or not you believe in an afterlife, you want to retrieve happy memories of your loved one instead of dredging up the last, sad moments shared, especially if they involve physical or mental illness.

Each time you catch yourself starting to think about the darker moments, quickly try to shift your thoughts to happier and brighter ones. Focus on your gratitude for having been able to share life with that person. It is like a mental game of tug-of-war—and believe me, it feels like it when you start doing it. You are training your brain to think in the present and to bring the past to the forefront only when it is positive. If you really feel the need, allow yourself time to revisit the sad memories, but make sure it is just a visit and not permanent residency.

This type of mental training worked well for us and was an integral part of our healing. If you are having difficulties getting out of the darkness and ugliness of your loss and much time has passed, seek professional help. There are many qualified counselors and therapists who can assist you.

Keep Your Vacations, Holidays, Traditions, and Celebrations

Your life has changed, but this does not mean you must stop living your best life possible or avoid doing things that used to bring you great pleasure. Keeping your vacations, traditions, and celebrations alive will foster healing. They may be different without your loved one, but they still have meaning and can bring you some comfort and happiness.

Vacations

Do not stop taking family vacations. You need the time away to rest and relax. Get out of your house and try something new. Now more than ever, you need something to look forward to and time to decompress. You can use a change of pace to get your mind off your loss. If places you used to visit bring back too many memories, then change them up a little.

As a family we used to go to the Northwoods in Hayward, Wisconsin, but decided it may be painful to return to that specific area, at least right now. We found a new place in Wisconsin to vacation. If you used to take cruises together, do something like switch up the cruise line or destination. Sometimes just a small modification is enough to make it more enjoyable for you and everyone else in your family. If you can't afford the time or money for an extended vacation, then try visiting new places near your home for a day or two.

Birthdays

Tom, Kelli, and I still celebrate Nick's birthday in some way that honors him. Most of the time we get a cake, sing "Happy Birthday," and try to do something we know Nick enjoyed doing. One year we went for vanilla milkshakes together because they were Nick's favorite and talked about our favorite memories of him. Another year we sat and reminisced about him in a park where he planted a little tree as a child. Birthdays are very hard at first, but they do get better with time. Try to make them celebrations of life instead of special days to mourn.

Holidays, Traditions, and Celebrations

If you have any holidays, traditions, or celebrations that were important to you before your loved one passed, it is healthy to continue them now, even though doing so may be painful at first. I believe your loved one would want you to keep what is meaningful to you. Each year this will get a little easier. You just have to trust me on this one.

We celebrate Christmas, and although I didn't want to decorate the first year, I pushed myself to do it. If I had been too sad and lacked the energy to do anything that initial year, I think it would have been perfectly understandable to skip celebrating, especially if Nick had passed right before the holiday. It was seven months after Nick passed, and I thought I could at least try to decorate. The hardest part was putting up our Christmas tree.

Every year since the kids were born, I would get a special ornament for each of them that symbolized their age and primary interest for that year. The plan was to give Nick and Kelli their ornaments once they grew up so they would have special reminders of their childhood to place on their own trees. Hanging Nick's ornaments, like "Baby's First Christmas," Barney, Elmo, piano, trumpet, and barbells, was difficult enough, but going through the *handmade* ones from his childhood was complete torture. Tom and Kelli didn't want to help for the first few years because they knew how painful it would be, and I respected their feelings.

I'm so glad I hung those ornaments on the tree, though, because although it was very painful in the beginning, each year got easier. I always made sure I had a funny movie playing in the background to lighten the mood, like *Elf* or *Christmas Vacation*. I think 2018 was the first year since Nick died that I actually enjoyed putting up the tree. Hanging the ornaments was a little bittersweet, but it was all painful not too long ago, so I'm making progress. I hope by the ten-year mark, the sweet will far outweigh the bitter.

Whether you celebrate holidays like Christmas, Hanukkah, or Kwanzaa, or take part in any other traditions, celebrations, or festivals, I encourage you not to abandon what means a lot to you. If doing exactly what you have done in the past is too painful, then make simple modifications that allow you to still feel comfortable.

Sending out holiday cards was a tradition we modified. After Nick passed, it was difficult to understand how to sign our cards and still honor him. People handle the card dilemma in various ways. There is no right or wrong way to sign cards after the death of a loved one. You have to find what feels right for you and your family. The idea of leaving Nick's name off the cards made me feel like I was wiping out his existence, but including his name with ours didn't feel right either. After much thought, I finally decided to include a note in our first holiday card after his passing with a one-time explanation of how I was signing our cards from that point forward.

I explained that I drew a tiny heart around the letter "N" following our signatures to symbolize that Nick will forever be in our hearts. I explained I will now always sign our holiday cards that way (I don't sign any other cards that way throughout the year) because I knew if Nick were here, he would wish everyone a Merry Christmas, and I believed he was doing so from the other side.

At first, I was a little nervous about sending holiday cards out that way, but much to my surprise, the response from our family and friends was overwhelmingly positive. Many have told me how much they love that I honor Nick every year that way, and I don't think they have said that just to make me feel better. With this simple modification, I am comfortable continuing a tradition that has always meant so much to me. If you have holidays, traditions, or celebrations that are painful now after the passing of your loved one, don't add to your loss by being too quick to give up what is important to you and what has brought you joy in the past.

Change the Room and Give Things Away When Ready

No rulebooks exist that dictate if, or when, you must change your loved one's room and give away his or her belongings. None. I wrote much of this book sitting at Nick's desk in his bedroom because I feel closest to him there. It is quite comforting. Over the past seven years, I have changed a few things in his room, but many of his belongings are still right there, like his framed posters on the wall, Cubs hat, and favorite ELO vinyl.

We gave away many of Nick's clothes when we were ready because we knew he would want others to get good use out of them, but we saved a few clothing items as reminders of him. I don't think there is anything strange about that. However, if we had made his room into a shrine, kept everything he owned, and had to touch or smell his clothes each day, then there might be a problem. If your attachment to your loved one's belongings is holding you back from moving forward and healing, then you may be stuck in the grief process and could benefit from reaching out for some professional help, joining a support group, or maybe both.

Confront Things That Might Get Weird

After Nick passed, I did not want anything to get weird. What I mean by that is, I didn't want any one thing to take on a substantial, dark meaning of its own and have some negative effect on me. If I sensed anything had that potential, I worked hard to nip it in the bud. For example, because I last saw Nick in Jamba Juice, I didn't want to associate that franchise with his death and feel bad every time I drove by one of those stores. So, I became proactive. About a month after Nick died, I called my girlfriend and asked her to go with me to the Jamba Juice in my hometown and just sit. I would have gone there every day until the weirdness went away because I was determined to flush out anything that could cause any adverse reaction from me. Fortunately, one time did the trick.

The dress I wore for Nick's high school graduation party was staring back at me in my closet one day. It reminded me of how much Nick worried about his party. It was taking on a whole life of its own, and I was not going to let it have that power over me. I took it out and kept wearing it until I got comfortable with it again.

For a while, college campuses evoked strong emotions in me because I was at the University of Minnesota when Nick died. When Tom and I started going on college visits with Kelli, painful memories flooded back to me during campus tours, making me break out in a sweat and my heart race. I didn't let Kelli know what was happening because she was excited to see the schools, and those visits were about her and her feelings for each campus, not mine. She didn't need to be reminded of her brother's death during such a happy time. I continued to go on college tours with her because I knew the more I did it, the easier it would get—and it did. Once again, I just had to work through it and not give up.

I'm not saying you have to push through everything right away, especially if something is upsetting you too much emotionally and physically. Take the time you need but understand that you may have to place yourself somewhere outside your comfort zone to get back into things. Find the balance. Be mindful of what is getting weird for you and, if you can, do not let it have power over you. Go into that store, wear that article of clothing, and walk that campus. Do what you need to do when the timing is right. If you need help getting past some hurdles, seek professional advice from a counselor or therapist.

Consider Alternatives to Mood-Altering Substances

Be careful to not rely on alcohol or any other mood-altering substances to make you feel better when you are grieving. Please do not be offended by my words or think I am preaching. I merely want to suggest that while you are grieving, you are extremely vulnerable and may think alcohol and other substances are the only ways you can get out of your pain and discomfort. The risk of these things becoming a crutch, or an addiction, is great under these new circumstances. Also, if you mask the pain and numb yourself with these things, you will just delay doing the work needed to heal and get back into the world again.

Grief is not like a broken bone. If you break your foot, you can take a painkiller to help with the pain and your foot will still heal. You don't need to feel the pain of your broken bone to heal. But with grief, feeling the pain of loss is an integral part of the healing process, and you cannot avoid it and still recover. I could not have numbed my pain with drugs or alcohol and still have had the clear mind necessary to come to terms with what happened to

Nick. Nor could I have done all the grief work required to function and integrate myself into somewhat normal life again.

I had to think straight to forgive myself and others for things we did or failed to do, including things we missed. I needed to be myself, unaltered by substances, so I could face people and figure out how to interact with them. I had to think of answers to tough questions about my son's suicide. Our family needed each one of us to be clean and sober so that we could help ourselves and one another through our grief, as well as work through our new family dynamic. It was hard work, but we had to face it head-on to heal.

If you start using substances to numb yourself from the pain, it may be difficult to stop because the pain is pretty constant, at least for the first year or two. Also, keep in mind that alcohol is a depressant. You may feel an initial high or numbing from it, but it will make you feel even sadder when the buzz wears off. It is all a very slippery slope, so I strongly recommend you choose some safer alternatives to help relieve your stress as you work through your grief, like the following:

❀ Exercise

❀ Play an instrument

❀ Listen to music

❀ Engage in a hobby

❀ Volunteer at a local charity

❀ Pray or meditate

❀ Spend time with pets

❀ Read books

❀ Watch television or movies

❀ Learn something new (take up a new instrument, sign up for a class)

Postpone Life-Altering Decisions

For the first few years after a loss or tragedy, you are in survival mode just trying to get through your pain. You do not think like you usually do. During this time, I recommend you postpone or at least identify and fully understand your motives before making any major decisions that can significantly affect your life, like moving, donating organs, joining the military, filing for divorce, or quitting a job, unless you had initiated that life event before your loss or tragedy.

Moving is a great adventure, but not if you are doing it to run away from someone or something like stigma. Organ donation and joining the military are noble if your motives are for all the right reasons, but not if they are an attempt to rid your guilt about something. You do not want to commit to anything based on a quick decision stemming from pain, discomfort, or guilt.

Sometimes marriages do not work out, and separation or divorce is inevitable, but marital problems after a loss or tragedy are way too common. Give your relationship the benefit of a few years to weather the storm of your situation. You do not want to rush into making any permanent decisions while you are grieving.

Quitting a job can be the fruitful beginning to a new career path, but you need to remind yourself that you are in a more fragile state than usual during the first few years after a loss. You may have less tolerance of others, patience, ability to relate, and ability to perform as you grieve, so consider giving yourself a one- or two-year grace period of healing before you make this type of life-altering decision.

If you choose to go ahead with any of these decisions, then, again, make sure you identify and understand the motives behind your actions.

Find Humor

What has happened to you in life is awful, of course, but do not let it change you to the point that you are bitter and cannot have fun or laugh after some time. If you see the humor in something, hang on to it for dear life because it is healing.

One day about five months after Nick passed, I was feeling sorry for myself. I decided to get out of my house and take a stroll to clear my head. As I was walking, I kept on going over in my mind all the difficult things I have had to endure in my life, how nobody truly understands how difficult it has been, and blah, blah, blah, blah, blah. Oh, I was the queen of my pretty little pity party of one. Suddenly, I heard someone enthusiastically yell, "Hi!" from across the street. I looked up and saw a young man who looked to be in his late twenties or early thirties in a motorized wheelchair riding down the sidewalk parallel to mine. He looked at me from across the street with a big smile.

As I walked over to him, I could see he had no use of his legs and almost no use of his arms because they were stiff, bent, and twisted. He was having a difficult time even keeping his head straight up while sitting. As I looked more closely, I recognized him. He was one of the greeters at the nearby Walmart who cheerfully welcomed me into the store one day with that same radiant smile. He asked me how I was doing today and was clearly delighted to make a new friend. I had a strong sense that this guy was thrilled to be alive.

I talked with my new friend, Craig, for about a half hour or so, and I walked away feeling uplifted from our conversation. He was a happy, kind, and lovely soul through and through . . . Man! Nothing like an optimistic, paraplegic-borderline-quadriplegic with a contagious zest for life to make you feel absolutely ridiculous for feeling sorry for yourself. As I walked back home, I just chuckled to myself and shook my head. I got the message loud and clear and laughed as I told God he had a real sense of humor and absolutely no subtlety whatsoever.

Humor exists in places least expected. As you can imagine, Tom, Kelli, and I are not big fans of bridges. Okay, I will admit it—we absolutely hate them. I can't even bear to watch the beloved Christmas classic *It's a Wonderful Life* anymore because George Bailey jumps off a bridge. I used to love that movie.

When making trips to and from Kelli's college, we had to cross over a bridge on one of the highways between our home and campus. Kelli and I nicknamed it the "Suck Bridge." For four years, each time Kelli was on the bus going to or from U of I, she would text me when she was on the Suck Bridge. I would do the same whenever I was riding shotgun in our car on the same route. We would add different funny emojis to our texts like the smiley with big eyes or the one that is a big pile of manure. We got pretty creative over her four years of college and even looked forward to opening each other's texts about that bridge. The bridge made us feel uncomfortable, so we lightened it up with some humor and made it a little fun thing between us.

These are the best tips I can give you for surviving loss. Again, what worked for me and my family may not work for you and yours, but they are worth considering. Please keep in mind that people, situations, and circumstance tend to change throughout the grief process, so you may want to circle back to these tips from time to time. A few that may not apply now, may later. I wish you much peace as you work through your loss. Keep hope because you *will* find the joy in life again.

Age 6, 2000

Age 18, 2012

College-bound with high hopes, 2012

Siblings and best friends, 2012

Family in Alaska, 2012

Chapter 16

Risk Factors and Warning Signs

E veryone should become familiar with the risk factors and warning signs for suicide because they are clues and red flares that save lives. Knowing the risk factors gives you the heads-up needed to look for warning signs, and if you are familiar with the warning signs, then you are more able to assess when to get professional and/or emergency help. I wish I had been familiar with more of the warning signs when Nick was alive because if I had recognized the ones I missed, maybe I would have been alerted to get Nick immediate help. Raise your awareness and learn the warning signs and risk factors. It is well worth your time, even if you don't think anyone you know has a mental health issue. You just never know if and when this information will become crucial in your life.

RISK FACTORS

If you type "risk factors for suicide" in any search engine, all kinds of sites will pop up that list many characteristics and conditions. People with an increased risk for contemplating suicide, attempting to take their life, or dying by suicide share some of these characteristics and conditions. Keep in mind, though, that many people who have some of these risk factors never attempt. Suicidal behavior is very complex and often difficult to predict. The following is a list of some of the most common risk factors:

- Mental health condition or disorder—clinical depression, anxiety, bipolar disorder, etc.
- Major physical health problem or illness
- Family history of suicide
- History of alcohol and/or substance abuse
- Loss (financial, social, relational, job, etc.)
- History of trauma or abuse
- Isolation and lack of social support (real or perceived)
- Prolonged stress (bullying, unemployment, relationship problems, harassment, death of a loved one, etc.)
- Easy access to lethal means (guns, drugs, bridges, pills, etc.)
- Exposure to other suicides (local, media, internet, etc.)
- Previous suicide attempts
- Hopelessness
- Impulsive and/or aggressive tendencies
- Inability to access health-care
- Unwillingness to ask for help due to stigma related to mental health

WARNING SIGNS

How can you tell if you or someone you know needs help? Warning signs are statements, behaviors, and symptoms that indicate a person may be thinking about taking their life and therefore signal help. Remember, there are no do-overs when it comes to suicide, so err on the side of safety and talk to someone (a mental health professional, another health-care provider, a parent, a teacher, clergy, or any other responsible adult) about what you are seeing or experiencing. The following are examples of some of the verbal, emotional, and behavioral warning signs for suicide:

Verbal

* Aren't I a burden? Everyone would be better off without me.
* I'm having a difficult time remaining positive. I have no more energy.
* I don't see a future with me in it. I don't see myself getting older.
* I want to kill myself. I want to die. I wish I could just leave this world.
* I feel trapped. I don't see a way out. Things will never change or improve. I have no more solutions. Nothing matters anymore.
* Things seem hopeless. I give up. I have no reason to live. I feel empty. Why should I even bother?

Emotional/Mood

* Depression
* Rage, irritability (constant or mood swings)
* Anxiety, agitation
* Humiliation, hopelessness, worthlessness, extremely low self-esteem
* Sudden change from sad/depressed to calm/happy (contentment after decision to die by suicide)
* Extreme guilt or shame
* Loss of interest
* Intense loneliness

- Resignation to circumstances, defeat
- Feeling tired or exhausted all the time
- Inability to focus, scattered thought pattern

Behavioral

- Withdrawing or isolating from family and friends
- Saying goodbye to family and friends
- Making the circuit to visit or call family and friends one last time
- Giving away cherished possessions (including pets)
- Increased use of alcohol or mood-altering substances
- Researching or looking for ways to end life (online, books, media articles, etc.)
- Making a suicide plan (stockpiling drugs, buying rope, buying a gun, etc.)
- Acting recklessly (driving vehicle with extreme speed, etc.)
- Taking extreme risks
- Sleep pattern disturbances
- Change in eating habits
- Personal hygiene neglect
- Frequent intense crying or crying episodes that are out of character
- Feeling unbearable pain (emotional, physical)
- Putting affairs in order (making will/trust, giving away safe-deposit box key, etc.)
- Sudden drop in grades, lack of interest in work, school, extra-curricular activities, or family

❈ Inability to complete assignments/tasks

❈ Trouble thinking, concentrating, remembering, and making decisions

❈ Seeking revenge

❈ Sudden and intense interest in death and afterlife (reading many books on suicide or near-death experiences)

Now that you are familiar with the risk factors and warning signs of suicide, let me share which ones I missed with Nick. This is painful for me, but I don't know a better way to show people that if you are not looking for these signs, you can miss them or brush them off as preteen/teenage drama or angst, regular hormonal changes, a midlife crisis, difficulties in accepting old age, or something else other than red flags for suicide.

I was not clueless when it came to matters of the mind. My undergraduate degree was in psychology, and I even completed one full academic year of postgraduate coursework in clinical psychology before going on to law school. With all this education, I still misidentified some of the clues. When they surfaced, I saw some of them but did not recognize them as being warning signs for suicide. I was not thinking in terms of my son possibly wanting to kill himself. None of my family did. And we are not alone.

Many people miss these signs or notice them but do not associate them as pointing to suicide because they love someone so much and want to see them in the best light. It sounds counterintuitive, but Tom, Kelli, and I were too close to Nick to understand that he was hurting to the point of wanting to end his life. And that is why I am sharing the worst part of our lives with you—because we do not want this to happen to anyone else. Know the risk factors and signs, and when you see the warning signs, act.

NICK'S RISK FACTORS

In hindsight, our family was able to see that Nick had some risk factors. He probably had a **mental health condition**, although he was not formally diagnosed with one. As discussed earlier, Nick may have had Asperger's (now considered part of the autism spectrum) and toward the end of his life, some type of depression. He mentioned two times in his last texts that he was depressed. Nick also may have had slight paranoia toward the end of his life. He perceived a **lack of social support** from his peers and prolonged stress from bullying, which is a type of **abuse**. Nick felt **hopelessness** and **defeat** at the end and was **unwilling to ask for help** due to the stigma attached to mental health. He had easy **access to lethal means** by attending a university located near high bridges. Another risk factor was that he felt **isolation and undue stress** because he questioned his sexuality and did not know where he fit in within society.

NICK'S UNWRITTEN WARNING SIGNS

It was painful to look back and recognize that more than a few of Nick's statements, behaviors, and emotions were warning signs for suicide. Hindsight can be gut-wrenching. He **gave away many of his clothes and other belongings** the summer before his senior year of high school. Another day during that summer, and while Tom was in the passenger seat, Nick **drove our car recklessly** on an expressway with such extreme speed that he got into an accident. The **loneliness and isolation** he felt throughout most of his life worsened in the later years of high school and college. Nick would often isolate himself from our family and stay in his room for hours, no matter how much we tried to get him to come out and join us to watch television or just sit with us. During the last few months of Nick's life, the warning signs increased. Again, my family pieced them together with hindsight as our guide. He repeatedly **told us he wanted to remain positive, but it was difficult.** He had two **episodes of crying** the last few weeks of his life, which was unusual for him. He exhibited a few **strange mood swings**, which was unlike him because he was always sweet and even-tempered.

After Nick died, we also realized that he made a point to **visit or see people one last time** in our family. His last time at home, which was spring break, he **did things he liked to do as a kid one final time**, like looking for stars with his telescope, listening to his favorite vinyls, and visiting the Museum of Science and Industry. During that break, Nick also seemed **unusually tired** and kept his **room messy**, which he never did. The last few months he experienced prolonged **stress** when the group of guys continuously strung him along about signing the apartment lease with him. Nick was also **stressed and humiliated** when the guys on the floor spread a rumor that he was gay, when he incorrectly thought the Jamba Juice girl viewed him as a stalker, and when I witnessed this misunderstanding. During the last few weeks, he even asked Tom and me on two separate occasions if we **thought he was a burden.**

NICK'S WARNING SIGNS IN TEXTS

Now let's take a closer look at Nick's last texts to me (provided in their entirety in chapter 3) and examine how some of these warning signs presented themselves. I hope this will help you identify warning signs in your communications with your friends and loved ones should they appear. The first text thread occurred ten days before Nick's suicide. The following are excerpts:

> It's just so hard . . . it seems like everyone leaves me out. I don't know why, and it really depresses me.

(Depression)

> I'm losing my old friends and can't make any close new ones. People are polite but leave me out of things. I give up. It's like no one cares. And it's taking its toll.

(Isolation, Hopelessness, and Resigned in Defeat)

> I don't know but I'm struggling. Why has it been so hard?

(Depression, Hopelessness, and Resigned in Defeat)

Clearly, there were signs here, but I thought Nick was depressed, not suicidal. Many parents receive similar types of texts or calls from their children the first year they move away from home to attend college or to start a new job. It's common for kids to have difficulties during that first year adjusting to independence.

When I suggested to Nick that he should go to the health center on campus if he needed to talk with someone, he responded, *Mom no. I'm almost done with school.* I thought this meant his issues were not bad enough to warrant immediate help because he didn't feel the need to talk to someone professionally during those last few weeks of classes. Remember, Nick was moving back home for summer in two weeks, and I planned to have him see a therapist as soon as he got home. Also, I assumed that because we had such a close relationship, he would have told me if his difficulties were severe enough to be life-threatening. We talked about everything, and Nick had always been honest with Tom and me, except for possibly that one time in high school when he told us he thought the psychologist "hit on him."

I tried to figure out how bad the situation was when I asked, *Are you going to be ok? How bad is it?* He responded, *I'll survive. I'm just trying to study.* However, now I know I should have asked Nick directly if he was having thoughts of suicide when he told me he was depressed. You can see how I tip-toed around this idea after I suggested to Nick that he could go to the health clinic if he needed to talk to someone. I said, *I'm not saying I think you need it by any means. I'm just saying the service is there if you need it.*

It's common for people to be afraid of asking others if they are thinking of killing themselves, or to even hint at it, because they don't want to hurt their feelings or lower their self-esteem by suggesting they seem not to be thinking right—and they certainly don't want to give them the idea to take their own lives. However, while conducting research for the Nick's Network of Hope website, I learned that asking people if they are suicidal does not plant the seed, making them become so.[1] They may not tell you the truth, but at least you created the opportunity for them to share with you if they are having those thoughts.

If your loved ones or friends answer yes, ask if they have a plan. If they say they are having thoughts of hurting themselves but do not have a plan, I think you must still get them professional help, immediately. That may mean even calling 911 if you live far away from them and don't know anyone who could take them for immediate assistance. Beware—do not be lulled into a false sense of security by thinking that if your loved ones do not have a plan, they have no serious intention of harming themselves. Plans can be made within a few minutes, so err on the side of caution and seek professional help.

Nick was honest and open enough to share with me that he was struggling but was not willing to tell me he was having thoughts of suicide. He assured me he would be okay. I think Nick may have done this out of love and because he didn't want to worry us. Nick always put the feelings of others first, especially his family. But this was a time he should have put himself first because he was having life-threatening difficulties. Nick should have reached out for help. I think he was trying hard to *stay* here and wanted to live but ultimately lost his battle because he was fighting a significant portion of it alone.

Now let's look at excerpts from the text thread between Nick and me that happened two days before his suicide. Nick texted me that Saturday morning and said:

❀ *Mom, I just had the worst day of my life yesterday. I need to call you right when I get off of work at probably 11. Please don't let this scare you. I'm managing but have had a few embarrassing and tough realizations to swallow lately. I'm trying to fight depression with all my might and don't know if I can stay here anymore. I'm doing my best. I'm studying. And I can't wait to go home.*

❀ *Basically, I'm starting to see how much stuff I've been left out of by people I thought were my friends. They've been trying to hide so much from me. And I finally got a glimpse why. And now it makes so much sense.*

He had been embarrassed (**humiliation**) by his peers and was telling me he was fighting **depression**. He said he didn't know if he could *stay* there anymore (which in hindsight could also mean he was struggling to stay here in this world—alive). He appeared to be **resigned in defeat**. He had felt isolated and betrayed by friends. Nick's statement "They've been trying to hide so much from me" may have been a sign of **paranoia**. What threw me off was when he said he didn't want the message to scare me. I took this to mean he was upset but tried to assure me it was not anything bad enough to be life-threatening. Once again, Nick was putting me first and trying not to worry me.

Tom, Kelli, and I do not blame ourselves for missing these signs—or for anything else. Sure, we did at first, as most loss survivors do in the beginning stages of grief; however, we moved past that stage. Also, we never pointed the finger at each other, not even right after the suicide. We all loved Nick and would have done anything for him.

Some people may read these texts and think we are complete fools for missing these warning signs because they seem obvious in black and white; however, it wasn't so obvious when it was happening. Life doesn't unfold quite that easily. What people need to understand is that when individuals help someone work through difficult times day after day, as many parents do with a child who struggles with social issues or any other significant challenges, then it can be difficult for them to know when a particular crisis is the last straw leading to suicide. They are deep in the woods putting out fire after fire. The warning signs become day-to-day behavior, not new flashes of caution. Families are sometimes too close to see the clues. This is why it is so important to speak up if you see warning signs from someone, especially if their family and friends are missing them.

If you are the person who is going through a crisis, you need to communicate with your family and friends if you are having thoughts of taking your life so they understand the urgency of the problem and can help you.

Learn the risk factors and warning signs. See the red flags in my last conversations with my son and put them all in your tool-box so you will be prepared to act if ever needed. Benefit from my family's painful hindsight and save as many lives as you can.

Chapter 17

Things to Know to Help Yourself and Others

I f you are struggling to find hope, please do not give up. A brighter future awaits you—really. If you reach out and get help, you can keep yourself alive and safe. You can start feeling better. As a mom who lost her son in such a needless way, I would love to give you a big hug, sit down with you, and tell you some of the things I wish Nick had understood during his life that could have helped him stay. Because that's not possible, I am sharing them here, with you in mind.

Some of these life truths stuck out for me after watching my son struggle, and one tip (the safety plan) I learned after Nick passed. Please remember that I'm a mom, not a mental health professional; nevertheless, I believe the truths and tips I am providing here are well worth your consideration.

Perhaps you are caring for someone in need other than yourself. I've included vital lessons I learned, once again through my experiences with Nick and after his suicide, that may prove helpful to you when trying to keep your friend or loved one safe.

If the people you want to help are suicide loss survivors and you're uncertain about what you can do to assist their recovery, I've recommended ways you can reach out to them and offer your support while still respecting their grief journeys.

THINGS YOU SHOULD KNOW
TO HELP YOURSELF

Make a Safety Plan

Write a plan for your safety when you are calm and thinking clearly. Do not wait until you are in a crisis to figure out what you need to help yourself feel better again and, more importantly, keep you out of harm's way. Involve someone you trust when making your plan so that person can help you implement it when necessary.

The following information may be helpful to include in your safety plan:

* Things you can do to help yourself feel better (work out, eat healthy, get enough sleep, play calming music, take prescribed medications, go to counseling, exercise, go to a support group, play with pets, etc.)

* Family members, friends, and health-care providers you can reach out to for help (include names, phone numbers, emails)

* Emergency numbers to call if you are in distress (include 911, national hotline phone and text numbers, nearby hospital numbers, etc.)

* Things to avoid if they make you feel worse (caffeine, alcohol, drugs, sad movies, looking at old pictures, watching the news, being around certain people, etc.)

* Reminders about why you should choose to keep living (names/pictures of people and pets you love, future goals to accomplish, things you most enjoy in life, etc.)

Whenever you feel like you are slipping into an unhealthy mode, take out your safety plan to remind yourself of the things you must do to keep yourself safe and feeling better, like contacting a therapist for treatment or calling upon friends or family members who can support you. It also makes sense to call the person who helped you create the safety plan because he or she is the most familiar with it and can help make sure you are implementing it as needed.[1]

Yell for Help and Then Allow It

Nick had a piano on his chest and could not breathe. His big mistake was failing to communicate clearly when attempting to yell for help. He also failed to allow anyone to help him. He could not lift the piano by himself because his depression and anxiety were too great. Nick did yell, to some extent, because he did tell me he was depressed on two different occasions right before he died, but he never said he was having thoughts of suicide. That part was too important to leave out.

Nick also told me his depression was not that bad when I suggested he go for help at the health-care clinic on campus. This implied to me that his issue was not life-threatening, and we could wait the two weeks it would take to finish the school year and get him home before seeking counseling. Why did Nick tell me his depression was not that bad and then kill himself soon after? One possibility is that Nick changed his mind about opening up to me about his depression, so he decided to pull back by brushing off how badly he was feeling.

I believe a more likely possibility is that Nick was having good days and bad ones at that time, and he really thought his depression wasn't so bad on that particular day when I asked. He was desperately trying to handle his depression, his stress, and everything else on his own and didn't want to worry anyone, especially our family. On his bad days, he contemplated taking his life but never told anyone, and on his good days, he tried to tell us (even himself) that things weren't that bad. We misinterpreted his warning signs because he was giving us mixed messages. He failed to clearly yell for help.

Be careful of this. If you are like Nick and are having good and bad days, and the bad days consist of you contemplating suicide, then you must get help for yourself so that you can stay safe. You need to tell someone what you are going through and specifically say to that person you are having thoughts of taking your life—even if these thoughts are only occurring every now and then. You must reach out and get help so that if you have another bad day and those suicidal thoughts are triggered, you have a safety net below you. Allow someone to help you.

Nick should have been more direct by yelling for help and explicitly communicating he was having thoughts of suicide. If Nick had told us, "I am depressed, *and* I have had thoughts of killing myself," then he would most likely be alive today. We would have known to keep an eye on him and get him the help he so desperately needed.

Nick did not have a safety plan because we had never heard of safety plans back then, and even if we had, I was not aware he needed one—but he did. If he had prepared a safety plan, then when he started feeling like the world was crashing down on him, he could have initiated the steps outlined in his plan. Nick could have called someone on his list, a hotline number, or urgent care, and he could have told people he didn't want to be alone because he had thoughts of taking his life.

Nick also could have yelled for help years ago when he saw the two psychologists in high school; however, he neither volunteered that he was having thoughts of suicide nor admitted to it when they asked him during their evaluations. Either he indeed wasn't suicidal at that time, or he felt he could not be honest with these doctors. We'll never know for sure, but in hindsight, Tom and I think Nick was suicidal because he gave away so many of his belongings. We even wonder if Nick chose to attend the University of Minnesota because he knew those bridges were there.

If Nick did have thoughts of suicide in high school and had shared those feelings with either of the psychologists, perhaps he would still be here today. They might have tried medications, therapy, or a combination that may have helped him and possibly even prevented his suicide in college. At the very least, our family would have known to watch him carefully.

If you are suffering from depression or some other mental health issue, or if you are having some crisis—whether it be health related, financial, relational, legal, or something else—*this is your piano.* Call 911 if you are having thoughts of suicide and need immediate help. You can also call the National Suicide Prevention Lifeline number, 1-800-273-TALK (8255). This Lifeline is a national network of local crisis centers that provides free and confidential support 24/7 for people in distress. It also offers prevention and crisis resources for your loved ones.[2] Again, you can call this number for yourself or to ask what you can do to help someone else you think might be suicidal.

The Nick's Network of Hope website (nicksnetworkofhope. org) has the National Suicide Prevention Lifeline number posted on several pages and contains additional information and links to valuable resources. In addition, our resources page contains many helpful links and phone numbers, including hotline numbers.

The takeaway here is to tell someone what you are going through by communicating clearly. If you are having thoughts of suicide, tell people *exactly that*, even if you are having good days mixed in with your bad days. If you need help, do not pull back and say you are doing well or make it sound like your struggles are no big deal when someone asks how you are doing or if you need assistance. Tell someone and then allow that person to help you. If that person doesn't assist you, immediately tell someone else until you get the help you need. Your life may depend on it—Nick's did.

And this is important—if you are in crisis or have a mental health condition, you may not be thinking like you usually do. Your mind may be telling you untruths like these: there is no hope in my situation; I am a burden to my loved ones; everyone would be better off without me; things will not improve over time; no one cares what happens to me; I will never make friends; my grades are too low to face my parents ever again; I can never live a happy life with this sexual orientation or identity; or I cannot live without that person in my life.

Don't let your mind trick you into believing these things because they are all false. You must tune out those negative thoughts and reach out and tell someone what you are thinking and how you're feeling. Do it on blind faith if you have to, and trust you will get better. Learn from my son and please reach out for help. Tell someone in a detailed, straightforward manner, leaving no room for doubt, if you are having thoughts of suicide, and then allow that person or others to help you. It is the most loving thing you can do for yourself, your family, and your friends.

Bullying and Other Mistreatment Are a Reflection of Them, Not You

If you are being bullied or mistreated in some other way, those actions against you are a reflection of your abusers, not you. That is true with no exception. Reach out for help and tell how others are treating you. Don't try to handle it alone. You, like everyone else in this world, deserve to be treated with kindness and respect.

You Are Not a Burden

No kid is a burden to his or her parents, and no other family member is a burden to anyone else. If you feel like you are a burden, please know that if given a chance, your family would do everything possible to assure you that you are not. I know from experience that if your family lost you, they would be living life with a crushing emptiness that can never be filled—talk about burdens. Please do not put your family, friends, and other people who care about you through that trauma and anguish. If someone in your life has, God forbid, told you that you are a burden, then know that statement is a reflection of his or her brokenness. It is not about you. You must *never* put that on yourself and believe you are a burden on your loved ones. If you are unable to trust this on your own, then please, please, please trust me on this one.

People Care More Than You Think

Nick did not think he had friends, but he did. Maybe his short-sightedness was due to his depression or some other mental illness, but the fact remains that more people cared for him than he ever realized—and it was like that his whole life. All the testimonies at his memorial mass were proof of that. When he died, he had just turned nineteen. The teenage years are stressful for everyone because hormones are all over the place, and kids are trying to figure out who they are and where the limits are in life. Most people get a whole lot nicer as they mature and settle down. If you think the people around you do not seem to care, then reach out further because kind people who want the best for you are all around you. Talk to your teachers, counselors, parents, coaches, scout leaders, coworkers, or anyone else who makes you feel comfortable. Hey, I would not be writing this book if I did not care about what happens to you.

You Have the Benefit of Time

Nick did not think he had the benefit of time, but we all do unless you have a terminal illness. Circumstances almost always change over time. What seems like an impossible situation now will very likely not be an issue in a year or two; nevertheless, when you are in the thick of things, it is often difficult to see beyond your current set of circumstances. Sometimes you just have to believe with blind trust that your problems will get better.

Nick could not see a positive future, but he did have options. He could have continued his education somewhere else if he was unhappy at the University of Minnesota. As I said before, Nick was considering transferring to a college closer to home. He also could have taken a year off school to regroup. Many kids need a gap year or two to change their plans or figure things out for themselves. There's no harm in taking a hiatus to consider your best options or get the care you need if you are feeling overwhelmed, overly stressed, or depressed. Nick also could have tried medications, therapies, or any combination to see if anything would help him. The point is, Nick could not understand he had both time and options. You do too. Reach out to someone who can help you see that.

Sexual Orientation and Gender Identity Struggles Get Better

I believe a significant contributing factor in Nick's decision to end his life was his struggle with his sexual orientation. He did not question his gender identity; in other words, he was born male and identified as being male. However, he was not sure of his sexual orientation and was questioning whether he was gay, straight, or asexual (not sexually attracted to either gender), although many other sexual orientations exist. Nick was not attracted to males or females and was most likely asexual, but he probably would have figured that out for sure with a little more time. Or if he already knew, those extra years might have helped him feel comfortable with who he was from birth and secure enough to live his life in alignment with his sexual orientation.

For the most part, as people mature, they treat others with a little more kindness and respect. Nick was a teenager when he died, which typically involves a pretty tough crowd of peers no matter who you are. Most adults would tell you their teenage years were difficult, and if given a chance, few would agree to redo those years. If Nick could have held on until early adulthood, I think he would have had fewer difficulties fitting in and would have been more accepted by his peers.

If you are struggling with your sexual orientation or gender identity, reach out to local LGBTQ communities for help. There are also many national organizations and reputable websites that have valuable resources to assist you, such as The Trevor Project (thetrevorproject.org), GLSEN (glsen.org), and GLAAD (glaad. org). Our Nick's Network of Hope website (nicksnetworkofhope. org) also contains information and resources for you. It sounds trite, but you need to hold on and *stay* because things really do get better with time.

What Nick Would Want You to Know

If Nick could, I'm sure he would tell you that he did not realize how final the decision was to take his life. No one can take back a suicide, and there are no do-overs or second chances. He would tell you that he missed his college graduation, his opportunity to have a career, his birthdays, and his family's celebrations. He also will never get married or have kids. He will never see his sister walk down the aisle or be a doting uncle to her children. He will never be able to hug his mom and dad as they get older. He no longer has opportunities to grow and learn from this life. I am very sure that if Nick could, he would do everything possible to encourage you to *stay*.

If Hope Is Lost, Reach Out to Others

Reading numerous attempt survivor stories and talking to many people who have lost loved ones to suicide has opened my eyes to many of the reasons people attempt suicide. There seems to be no single cause; however, the one common denominator in most cases is a loss of hope. No hope for things such as being able to see how a problem can go away, an ailment will improve, a financial crisis will pass, a social situation will get better, a lifestyle will be accepted, pain from trauma will cease, or a relationship will mend. Generally, the person cannot envision a good future for themselves. If you are feeling hopeless right now, please reach out to others who can help you see the hope in your future again. We're all here to love and support one another, so go ahead and lean on others if you do not have the strength to stand on your own. Hope is there for you—let others help you find it again.

THINGS YOU SHOULD KNOW TO HELP OTHERS IN PAIN

Helping others who are struggling with life challenges or mental health issues, such as depression or anxiety, can be very challenging because you are continually trying to take care of their needs when they are in crises. You rarely have time to sit and research what to do and how best to help. Allow me to share the following lessons I have learned through my experience caring for Nick and after he passed.

It's Okay to Ask If Someone Is Having Thoughts of Suicide and an Exit Plan

I mentioned this before, but it is worth repeating here. It is okay to ask people if they are having thoughts of suicide. Research has shown that this question will not give them the idea to do so or push them to do anything self-destructive.[3] If they say they have had those thoughts, the follow-up question should be, "Do you have a plan?" Here, I mean a plan for how they would kill themselves, not a safety plan. Having thoughts of suicide, even with no plan, is cause for concern and still requires professional help.

Too often, people think that having no plan means that people contemplating suicide are not serious or are just trying to get attention. They are lulled into a false sense of security by thinking there will be plenty of time to get help. A plan, however, can be made within minutes, so it is crucial to take all thoughts of suicide very seriously. Also, keep in mind that when people are brave enough to admit they are having suicidal thoughts, sometimes they do not want to divulge having a plan because they know it will trigger an intervention by their families and friends.

Never leave people who are having a crisis alone. Call 911 immediately. Take them to the nearest emergency room for professional evaluation and intervention. For safety purposes, if they have used drugs or alcohol, tell the paramedics and emergency personnel right away so they can administer the proper urgent care.

Listen, Ask Open-Ended Questions, and Don't Try to "Fix"

A common gripe among married women is that after complaining to their husbands about something, they want to jump right in and "fix" the problem instead of listening and making their wives feel heard. We all do this to one another to a certain extent, including parents when their children bring them their problems. I know I often did this with Kelli and Nick. I asked all the questions I thought were needed to understand my call to action, but there were times those questions were not open-ended or directed to listen and learn how the kids were being affected by the situation at hand. Asking open-ended questions allows respondents to explain what they are feeling inside.

If people come to you and share that they are going through difficulties or suffering from depression, anxiety, or anything else for that matter, really listen to what they are telling you. Ask them open-ended questions like, "How are you feeling?" "What types of things are you experiencing?" "When do you feel that way?" "How often do you feel like that?" "How can I help you?" After asking these questions, sit forward and listen. Let them know you care and have heard them. Even if you disagree with what they are saying or how they are delivering their messages, recognize that those emotions are real. You do not want to shut down the lines of communication. Keep them talking and listen. Get immediate professional help if needed.

Do Not Be a Cheerleader When People Need Help

If your loved ones or friends are hurting and need help, it is always best to first assess the situation by asking questions. If you determine they are having a bad day, then being a cheerleader and encouraging them to push on and look at the glass as half full might be exactly what they need. However, if they are going through something more serious than one or two bad days, then they most likely need more than mere encouragement. Sometimes you can't cheer someone past their pain.

In our last texts, I told Nick how wonderful he was and that he was down to four weeks before the dorms would close for summer. I even told him that with pain there is personal growth. I was trying my best to lift his spirits by being supportive and encouraging, but Nick needed more because he was not just having a bad day, or series of days. Giving someone only encouragement when they need more can be dangerous, especially if he or she is going through major depression or some other mental health issue. It's like throwing a drowning person a rubber ducky when they need a life preserver.

With the benefit of hindsight, I now understand Nick needed me to intervene and get him help. There were many options. If I would have known he was in a crisis, I could have immediately called 911. I could have contacted local authorities in Minnesota to do a wellness check to assess the situation if I was still in Illinois. I could have called the college and arranged for someone to stay with Nick and carefully keep an eye on him while I flew out to be by his side. He needed immediate, professional help, but I did not realize it. None of my family did.

We have learned to not beat ourselves up for things missed because we were trying our best and dealing with extraordinary circumstances. Hindsight is painful and truly 20/20, so please use our hindsight in any way you can to save your loved ones.

Believe the Behavior More Than the Words

If your loved ones or friends tell you that they are not having thoughts of suicide, but all their behaviors point in that direction (look again at my list of warning signs), believe the behaviors you see more than what they tell you. Sometimes it is okay to believe actions more than words. Why? Your loved ones or friends may be trying to protect you by not telling you how they feel to spare you the worry; they may truly think they are all right but may be incorrect; they may feel they are a burden and want to save you from having to handle one more problem; or they may want to try to stay positive, or for your sake, at least appear positive. I imagine there are even more reasons than these.

Nick told me he was struggling but was okay. He assured me he didn't need to talk with someone at the on-campus health center. I took him at his word, but his behavior did not match what he was telling me. I should have believed his behavior and not his words. It is a hard thing to do when the person—especially someone you love and trust—is assuring you they are doing fine. You may be afraid they will think you don't believe them, but that is okay. It is better to keep them safe.

If Significant Difficulties Exist, Stay Close

As a mom whose son took his life while away at college, I would be remiss not to include this tip. If you notice that your loved ones are having significant difficulties or struggling more than most with basic life challenges, consider keeping them somewhat nearby so you can be more available whenever they need you. If your loved ones insist on moving away for something like a job or school, encourage them to relocate no farther than a distance you can travel by car, roundtrip, in one day. Not having to take an airplane or long car ride allows you to visit them more and assess how they are adjusting to their environment.

Phone calls, FaceTime, and Skype are effective forms of communication, but there is nothing quite like being present in person to assess a situation. Face-to-face visits allow you to see things like how your loved ones interact in their environment, including how people in their circles treat them. You can assess their appearance and the condition of the dorm room, apartment, or home. Look for poor personal hygiene, an empty refrigerator, pulled blinds, excessive garbage, empty bottles everywhere, and things in complete disarray (more than ordinary neglect). Proximity is no guarantee for safety, but I think it gives you a better chance of keeping your loved ones safe.

When Nick went to the University of Minnesota, he was about six and a half hours away. We did not see him every month, so it was difficult to gauge how he was adjusting to living away from home for the first time. We'll never know if living closer to us would have saved Nick, but we would have had more opportunities to observe how he was doing. Whenever he felt sad, lonely, invisible, or betrayed by others, we would have been close by for him to come to us. I believe receiving our love and emotional support in person on a more regular basis would have made a big difference in Nick's emotional well-being.

During one of our weekly calls with Nick, he mentioned how he had underestimated the benefit of living near family when he decided to attend a college so far away. Interestingly, when Kelli began her college search, Nick told her to choose a school that wasn't too far from home.

Now granted, this is one boy's opinion, and he was going through a lot. Certainly, many kids thrive moving far away from home and love the opportunity to become more independent, taking greater responsibility for their lives. People need to weigh it all and evaluate each case carefully, especially if the person moving away seems to need a network of support.

THINGS TO HELP SUICIDE LOSS SURVIVORS

Sometimes it is difficult to know how to help someone grieving, especially if their loved one died by suicide. As a suicide loss survivor, and someone who has spoken to many other loss survivors,

I can tell you that the kindness, understanding, and support of our family and friends is an integral part of how we work through our grief and rebuild our lives. We have gone through something extraordinarily difficult. We need you. Consider these tips to help, support, and comfort the loss survivors in your life.

Do Not Avoid

Even if you think you do not have the right words to say, reach out and let the survivors know you care. They need your support. If you cannot do that in person, then at least send a card or note. Texting is usually an excellent way to reach out to someone, but under these circumstances, a form of communication that is a little warmer and more comforting would be better, at least initially. If you do text, follow up with a more personal method of communication.

Listen but Do Not Compare or Try to Fix

Be there to listen to the survivors talk about their heartbreak, but understand you cannot take away their pain. Grieving is a process that includes learning how to live with the loss. Give survivors the time and space they need to do that work. Please do not compare their grieving to anyone else's because everyone grieves differently and at their own pace. Their loss will never completely go away, but with time, they will figure out how to live with it. Support the survivors through their entire journey of learning how to move forward.

Remember Loved Ones and Talk about Them

Survivors do not want the world to forget their loved ones, so talk about them. Don't worry that you may make them emotional by doing so. They would rather get choked up or cry than not be asked about their loved ones. Even through tears, they appreciate you remembered. Share fond memories, remember birthdays and anniversaries, and let them know you will never forget their beloved. If you never met their loved ones, it is okay to ask questions and show an interest in learning more about them. I love when people share their pleasant memories of Nick with me. I don't want them ever to forget him.

Allow Them to Work through Each Birthday and Anniversary of Passing

Each year the loved one's birthday and the anniversary of passing will get a little easier, but these two days will always be challenging, no matter how many years have passed. Especially in the beginning, they can be downright tough because they are reminders of the survivor's loss and pain, as well as their loved one's past pain. Some survivors want to be around others on these days, while others want to be left alone to deal with their emotions. As these days approach, reach out to the survivors in your life and let them know you care. Ask them how you can help ease their pain. Some survivors may not know what they want to do for those special days until the very last minute, so be patient and follow their lead.

These insights gained from my son's life and death are now yours. The most important thing to remember is that we *can* help ourselves, and we *can* help each other. Sometimes when life gets too busy or difficult, we lose sight of the fact that we are all connected. We must look out for one another and help whoever we see struggling to help themselves. Those who are having problems need to reach out and clearly communicate their need for assistance. We can offer each other help, hope, and comfort—and we can save lives.

Chapter 18

A Better and
Safer Tomorrow

M any people struggle with mental health issues today, and for myriad reasons, more and more choose to end their lives. Bullying and unkindness are commonplace in all areas of life, including our schools, workplaces, social circles, and governments. People are overworked and highly stressed, leaving some to openly take their frustrations out on others. There is a marked upswing in signs indicating this, such as gun violence, road rage, hate crimes, and vitriol spewed over social media. All kinds of professionals, agencies, task forces, and programs are working to help alleviate this vast array of problems, but there is no quick fix, easy solution, or one-size-fits-all diagnostic or treatment plan.

So, what can we do? We cannot just give up hope because the difficulties today appear too large or beyond repair. If we want even a fighting chance at spreading kindness and slowing down the ravages of mental illness, suicide, and some of the other current concerns, then we all need to get involved. All of us, young and old, need to look outside ourselves and ask, "Who around me needs help? Do I know someone at home, school, work, or anywhere else I go who seems to be hurting? Is there anyone in my life who needs to hear that someone cares? Is there someone being picked on who needs an ally? Do I know anyone who looks lonely or resigned?"

If someone comes to mind, then we have to take action. This may require us to take time out of our busy days or push ourselves outside our comfort zone. We need to tell these people that we recognize they may be hurting and ask them how they are doing. Then, we have to listen—I mean *really* listen—to what they have to say, let them know we heard what they said, and show them we care. If everyone starts showing this type of kindness and compassion for others, it will go a long way. It may help someone's depression and show someone who may be lonely and contemplating suicide that people do care about their well-being.

We can do even more. Allow me to share with you some ways I think we can promote kindness, decrease pressure on people, lessen the occurrence and impact of mental health issues, and even prevent suicide. If we want a better and safer world, then we must implement these ideas comprehensively, consistently, and universally. We cannot just have some communities carry out a few of them here and there. We all have to commit to doing the work.

GATHER INFO FROM AS MANY ATTEMPT SURVIVORS AND LOSS SURVIVORS AS POSSIBLE

We need to continue talking to as many attempt survivors and loss survivors as possible because they are crucial to figuring out how we can slow the escalating rates of suicide. The big glitch here is that all suicides and attempts are traumatic and have stigma attached. For these reasons, most attempt survivors and loss survivors are unwilling to share their stories. However, the more we destigmatize mental health issues and emphasize the need and importance for these survivors to come forward, the greater the chance they will step up and teach us what they have learned through their experiences.

We all go through difficulties and challenges in life. But what happened to the attempt survivors and the loved ones of loss survivors that made their pain so unbearable they wanted to end it all? Were the difficulties and challenges more extreme than most of us face? Did they suffer from some mental or physical illness that made them more vulnerable than most? If so, did they have a predisposition for that illness? Did some trauma, such as sexual abuse, divorce, crime, or war conflict cause or add to their inability to continue with life? Was that trauma ever identified and addressed? What treatment did they receive for that trauma? What were their breaking points, and how did they know when they reached them?

Attempt survivors can teach us what helps them *stay* here after their attempt. Are they in therapy, do they take medications, or is there something else that helps them feel better? What works for them? What doesn't? Do they have safety plans? At what point do they recognize in themselves that it is time to use their plans? In the past, what ways did our mental health system work for them, and did it ever fail? If so, how?

In preparation for writing this book, I searched the internet for suicide attempt stories. They were not easy to find due to the stigma and pain involved for survivors to open up and talk about their experiences. I did, however, discover one website that contains over a hundred and fifty suicide attempt stories, livethroughthis.org. The author, a suicide attempt survivor herself, interviewed and photographed all one hundred–plus survivors. They courageously agreed to come forward and share their stories online, using their real names and portraits to help destigmatize mental health. It was important to these survivors to show readers that the faces behind mental health issues look like you and me.

These stories give the world an inside look at some causes that lead to an attempt, ways we can improve our mental health system, resources that help attempt survivors *stay* in this world (how to use a safety plan, where to find hope, what treatments help, etc.), continuing challenges they face, and much more. I encourage you to read as many attempt stories as you can find on the internet and elsewhere. It was time well spent for me because not only was it eye-opening, but it also helped me gain even more empathy and compassion for people who suffer from various life difficulties, like mental health issues.

Here are, in my opinion, the five most important things I learned from reading suicide *attempt* survivor life stories:

1. Mental health issues often, but not always, start at a very young age.

2. People who suffer some trauma and later attempt suicide often get put on medications; however, many times, the underlying trauma is overlooked and left untreated. The trauma must always be addressed and treated.

3. People attempt suicide for a variety of reasons, but almost all seem to feel some unbearable pain and loss of hope.

4. People who attempt suicide look like a cross section of society—just like everyone else. Mental health issues and life struggles affect people in all walks of life.

5. Safety plans *really do* help suicide attempt survivors keep themselves healthy and get them back on track if they start feeling overwhelmed or believe they are slipping into a crisis.

We can also learn much from suicide *loss* survivors (again, these are people like me who have survived the suicide of a loved one). I have spoken to, and worked with, many suicide loss survivor families over the past several years. When I asked them to tell me about their loved ones, these are the five most common observations they shared:

1. They were in deep pain but often tried not to show it.
2. They felt they were burdens and that everyone would be better off without them.
3. Near the end of their lives, they had difficulty focusing and concentrating.
4. When they experienced happier times, they were passionate about life.
5. They seemed to be old souls (older and wiser than their physical age) and were very sensitive.

These are just a few of the critical things we can learn from suicide loss and suicide attempt survivors. The more stories that are shared, the more we can learn about mental health and suicide.

As a side note, I, together with many suicide loss survivors I have spoken with since Nick died, would like to encourage people to modify one phrase commonly used in the mental health community. Instead of saying, "Suicide is *always* preventable," we encourage others to say, "Suicide *can be* preventable." We understand the good intent behind using the word "always"; however, many suicide loss survivors will tell you that sometimes you can offer help to someone and do all the right things, but that person still decides to take his or her life.

Saying suicide is "always" preventable makes the family members, health-care providers, and anyone else who cared for a person who died by suicide feel like failures and stigmatized despite their best efforts. The phrase "suicide *can* be preventable" still sends a valuable message without causing more pain for the loss survivors.[1]

LESSEN THE PRESSURE WE PUT ON OUR YOUTH

What Is the Pressure?

Pressure on our youth comes from a lot of places: schools, social media, coaches, peers, parents, and even the kids themselves. This pressure causes too many kids to take their lives. Again, it is the second leading cause of death for people ages ten to thirty-four.[2] Now is the time to make changes in how much pressure we put on our kids before we senselessly and tragically lose any more. Let's first talk about the types of pressure from the top of the educational system downward. (I apologize in advance for overusing the word *pressure*, but in this case, synonyms are not adequate substitutes and seem to minimize the force on our kids today. So, let's just call it what it is.)

Pressure in High School

As a parent who went on many college visits with my kids, I know for sure that some of the pressure comes from colleges and trickles down to high school students. We toured many college campuses as a family and always tried talking to someone in each admissions office. Some admissions officers seemed well aware of the pressure we all put on our kids through the college admissions mania, but many were cold—even snooty—as they told us the standards for admittance to their schools.

I walked away from several of those visits frustrated, even a little angry, that somehow, we all lost sight of the fact that most college applicants are only eighteen years old. At eighteen, you are not supposed to be perfect, have a well-balanced resume, or know exactly what you want to do for the rest of your life. Some colleges are more covert than others when expressing these expectations, but the message is still there, and the prospective students know it.

You don't even have to step foot on a college campus to feel that type of pressure, though. High school guidance counselors help kids learn the criteria needed for college acceptance and introduce them to resources that specialize in admittance statistics, like charts that break down the percentage of kids accepted in past years within each range of grade point averages. High schools want *their* kids to be competitive in the college admittance process, so they encourage rigorous high school academic schedules and activities for their students, as well as high scores on the ACT and SAT.

Many high schools even promote their school publicly by using their students' Composite ACT scores. A high school in my hometown posted on its website that the Composite ACT score for their students averaged 28 or higher for fourteen consecutive years. High schools often compete with each other districtwide by using test scores.

The students internalize all these societal and educational standards, expectations, and statistics, making it almost impossible not to feel pressure to perform. And when the parents of college-bound kids find out what it takes to get into certain colleges and the rigors of the application process, many succumb to the pressure and do whatever it takes to ensure that their kids will be competitive among the rest of the applicants. Hell, we have even had celebrities succumbing to the pressure by cheating and buying their kids' admissions into colleges.

Many parents go into hyperdrive and "encourage" their kids to do things like stay focused, take hard classes, be on the best sports team, do volunteer work, and sign up for all other kinds of activities. Then they go to all the sports games with their kids, drive them to tutors, help them with homework, sign them up for private lessons, and research and schedule their child's next best opportunity.

When their kids lose focus, get a bad grade, or want to quit something, the parents remind (even nag) them they need to do well and need those activities to have the best shot at getting into a good college. Most parents do this out of love and to help their children get ahead, but to kids, it all equates to more pressure. As I said before, I'm not casting stones at any other parents because Tom and I fell into some of these same traps time and time again.

Those kids not planning to attend college have just as much pressure on them. If they attend a high school where the majority of kids go to college, they often feel pressure from teachers and other students for not taking that same path. Many times, they wind up being in the same curriculum as their college-bound peers and must complete the same assignments and attend the same events, as if they were planning for college. For example, some high school English courses require all students, even if college is not the goal, to write college application essays. Likewise, some schools mandate that every student take the ACT or SAT.

Often these kids feel like they are disappointing their parents and teachers by not going to college, especially if compared to their college-bound siblings. Some join the military when they graduate to get an education, and some cannot attend college because their parents expect them to get one or two jobs after high school graduation to help pay bills. I have spoken to kids who were expected to help their parents meet the mortgage payments for their family home. These young adults feel like they have the weight of the world on their shoulders.

Then there are those kids who want to go to college but do not have the aptitude or grades to get accepted, and others who have no interest in college because their talents do not require a college education to achieve their career goals. All these kids are still under pressure to make good grades and gain valuable experience because they need to be competitive in the job market right out of school, which is stressful in any economy. As if that isn't enough, they may have to find insurance, pay bills, buy cars, and find places to live. No wonder kids are so stressed out.

Having said all this, I would be remiss if I did not recognize the kids in schools who just want clean clothes on their backs and food to eat at lunch, let alone worry about grades. They often attend schools with substandard curriculums, underqualified teachers, and a lack of supplies. The basics many kids take for granted are either not as readily available for them or unobtainable. There are many types of pressure, and these kids feel it from all directions.

Pressure in Grade School and Middle School

From the time kids are in grade school, many parents learn what it takes to get them into honors classes. Typically, the prerequisites involve a minimum-high score on standardized tests and a minimum grade requirement. Even if the parents do not communicate these prerequisites to their children, most kids are astute enough to pick up on how their parents want them to perform. They know their parents want them to be in honors classes throughout grade school and middle school because then they will have a better chance of getting into the honors and Advanced Placement

(AP) classes in high school. It follows then, that if they do well in those high school classes, earn good GPAs, and achieve high AP test scores, they have a better chance of getting into a top college. They feel the pressure of trying to save their parents money for tuition and know they can do this if they achieve high AP test scores, earn college course credits, or earn scholarships. It is like sitting in a pressure cooker playing a long, drawn-out game of academic dominoes that all begins in grade school. Does any of this sound familiar?

Pressure of Sports in Middle School and High School

I think we can all agree that middle school and high school sports teams have changed a lot over the years, with an increased amount of pressure on kids today. Many coaches and parents push their kids harder and harder, as evidenced by the increase in youth sports injuries. Recently, I spoke with a twenty-two-year-old man who broke his back more than once playing high school sports and is still suffering from those injuries. He told me he suffered severe depression for a few years because of his injuries and even contemplated suicide at one point. Too often, student athletes are prescribed opioids to relieve pain from their sports injuries, adding to the opioid crisis of today.

How many times have you passed by a school and witnessed a practice or game held on a weekend—even Sundays? Some kids do not get any downtime. Sure, some athletes want to be on the team for the sake of the sport, and they love the commitment and rigors of team training and competition; nevertheless, far too many kids are on teams for other reasons. They may want that experience so they can add it on college applications, compete for athletic scholarships, gain admittance to colleges through sports, or simply make their parents happy. This is all pressure.

240

How to Lessen the Pressure

So how do we start lessening the pressure on our youth? Well, I think first and foremost, change has to start in our homes. Parents need to take a close look inward and evaluate if and how they put pressure on their kids because they probably have no idea they do so. They can't be afraid to sit down and ask their children if, when, and how they put pressure on them.

Of course, most parents act out of love and just want to help their kids. They want them to be well-rounded individuals with bright futures. They feel it's their responsibility to identify any untapped talents their children may have, so they sign them up for music lessons, dance lessons, science camps, and all kinds of sports. They expose them to different languages at a young age and all other types of programs.

If this sounds familiar, you may want to ask yourself the following questions: Are my kids always busy? Am I continually running them from one activity to another? Do they have any downtime to be kids and play? Do they have time just to sit quietly and use their imaginations? Do we take the time to eat our dinner together without rushing? Do my kids eat many meals in the back of the car as I drive them to their activities? Do I take time to sit down and ask my kids about their day and really listen to what they have to say? Do I want my kids to be in certain activities way more than they do?

We can lessen the pressure by telling our kids we are happy with—*and accept*—who they are now, instead of implying we will be pleased with them once they accomplish the next goals we set for them. This takes more living and loving in the present. We must keep in mind that kids are not small versions of ourselves, even if they look like us. They are not here to fulfill the goals we were unable to accomplish in our own lives, and we shouldn't look to our kids for a second chance at our youth. They are unique with their individual wants, talents, and dreams. If we embrace how they differ from us, then we can learn from those differences and expand our mindsets. We can learn from each other.

I think most older parents would tell younger ones that in hindsight, most of the things they worried about when their kids were growing up wound up not mattering. My friends and I often discuss how if we had to do it all over again, we would be way more "chill." It did not matter that our kids took as many honors classes as they did. They could have done well in any number of colleges, programs, and jobs even if they did not get accepted to the ones that required that type of curriculum. They didn't need to do half the clubs and activities they did throughout school. Of course, it was good for them to be involved in a few extracurricular activities, but the whole purpose is for those activities to *enrich* their lives, not cause undue pressure.

So, learn from us older parents and encourage your kids to have reasonable schedules. Do not get sucked into the academic dominoes game I discussed earlier. Resist strategically planning for their futures while they are still in grade school. Let their talents come out naturally without pushing them through their youth. Take the time to enjoy your kids while you have them because eighteen years go by quickly. Trust me, the physical and mental health of your kids is much more important than anything else.

One of the best lessons you can teach your kids is how to take on challenges and new opportunities while maintaining balance in their lives. While they still live under your roof, show them how to pull back on their schedules whenever they lose that balance and become too stressed. This is a skill they will need over and over throughout their lives.

We can also lessen pressure on our kids by how we define success, meaning, and satisfaction in our lives. We cannot tell our kids they can obtain these things only when they graduate from a top-tier college, get a high-paying job, make a lot of money, buy a big house, or drive a fancy car. Instead, we need to coach them to understand that success, meaning, and satisfaction in life will come when they do things like find the balance between family time and work, contribute positively to society, and believe in something bigger than themselves. It is good, of course, to teach our kids how to value and manage money at a young age, but they need to know money alone will not bring them happiness, nor will material objects.

Parents can also lessen pressure on their kids by respecting who they are and what they want to do in life. Love and accept your kids, whether they desire to attend college, learn a trade, or pursue some other dream. We all have different aptitudes, talents, and interests. Embrace whatever gifts your children possess. We need people in all kinds of trades, professions, and arts to make our society whole and the world a better place.

Also, love and accept your kids—and all people—whether they are gay, straight, asexual, or some other sexual orientation, and no matter their gender identification.

For those parents having difficulties accepting their child's sexuality and lifestyle, allow me to try to help by having you briefly imagine a role reversal. If you are straight, what if your parents had told you that you had to be gay, and they would accept you *only* if you were gay and lived a gay lifestyle? That sounds absurd, right? Why? Because you were born straight. Well, think about that for a moment. Why would someone choose to live a life where they have difficulties being accepted by the majority of others and have to fight for rights that most of us take for granted? Did you choose to be straight? No, right? I knew from the time I was five and kept pushing my rug next to Timmy Howell's during kindergarten nap time that I was a straight female, and no person or thing could have changed my mind. It was not a choice. It was not a moral decision. It was not a political statement. It was not an action for or against my parents. It was not a call for attention. It was nothing other than . . . I was born straight.

I was born in a female body, identified with being female, and was sexually attracted to males. There are, of course, people who are born male, identify as being male, and are sexually attracted to females. Anything other than these two combinations is where some of us become less understanding and accepting. Please try to be open to the possibility that people can be born something other than straight, and some can be born into a body of one gender but be another gender on the inside.

Why would anyone be prejudiced against someone for the way they were born? Another Law of the Universe: we don't get a vote on how we are born. Maybe we are all created differently so that we can learn to accept one another and live in harmony? What lessons would we acquire if we all looked and acted alike? None of us would grow as human beings, and the world would be a pretty dull place. I don't know about you, but when I was a kid, I never used just one crayon to make drawings because you could never do much with one color. But remember how excited we got if someone gave us that jumbo 120-box of crayons with all the different shades? Our drawings suddenly seemed to come alive with depth and beauty as we expanded our color palette.

If you are having difficulties in your relationships with family members, friends, and other people you care about because they are something other than what you expect them to be, then I encourage you to try to understand that their lives, and your relationships with them, are way more important than anybody's views. Agree to disagree if you must, but love and respect those people—and all people. We all deserve that in life . . . and lives may depend on it.

As for how to decrease the stress level on our kids that comes from our academic institutions, I am at a loss. I am not sure how to change the system that exists today in these institutions, especially at the college level, because I do not work in that area. I don't know how to lessen the expectations on kids if they want to get into a major university, but I do know it must be changed. I have hope and do believe that many excellent college administrators, professors, and deans are aware of all these problems and are committed to trying to find solutions.

There are also many compassionate principals, counselors, teachers, and other administrators at the high school, middle school, and grade school levels who are working hard to lessen the unnecessary pressure on their students, wherever and whenever they can, and are creating supportive learning environments. We need everyone else to get on board and do the same. I bet many who work in these school systems feel pressure to keep up with the college admissions mania that looms over all of us and are unhappy about it.

It is wise to encourage kids to work hard and do their best, but schools and parents need to carefully gauge how much they talk about topics like grade point averages, honors and AP classes, national test scores (including ACT and SAT), National Merit Scholarships, and job resumes. Having conversations about these subjects with students is, of course, necessary, helpful, and motivating, but they cannot be constant. Overdoing it causes kids to view these things not as goals but as impending threats to their futures. Administrators, teachers, and counselors of all schools, as well as parents, need to step back and reconsider when, where, and how often to talk about these topics because we're losing too many kids to suicide. Something has to change. I'm just a mom, but all this seems to be a good start.

CREATE A MOVEMENT TO TEACH KINDNESS, COMPASSION, EMPATHY, INCLUSION, AND OTHER WAYS TO BE HUMANE

There is hope for a future filled with kinder and happier people who enjoy life and each other, but we have to reboot as a society and go back to the basics of caring about one another. From playgrounds to Senate hearings, we have to stop and reflect on how we behave because we cannot continue as we do today with so many people treating others unkindly. It's unhealthy for everyone, even the innocent bystanders. We have allowed the goodness in our humanity to fade.

So how do we get back what we have lost? A good start is to make sure every child, at the earliest age possible, is educated about mental health and is taught virtues like kindness, compassion, empathy, and inclusion. Not only will we be forming a new generation of kindhearted people who are both self-aware and caring, but it will allow the rest of us the opportunity to reflect and make sure we are living by these virtues as well. We are role models for the generations to follow.

Families, schools, and communities need to work as partners to teach our children how to treat one another with kindness and respect, be sensitive to the feelings of others, recognize when someone is hurting, tolerate the differences of others, and much more. Then with a little time and guidance, the younger generation will not only treat each other with kindness and respect, but also demand that others do the same; not only know to act when someone is in need, but also strongly desire to help; and not only tolerate differences, but also fully appreciate diversity. In light of all the bullying, mental illnesses, suicides, hatred, and violence we see today, this needs to be more than a call to action—it needs to be an active movement: one on a large scale that involves *all* our communities, schools, and municipalities.

One example of a smaller movement that exists is the World Kindness Movement, an international effort to project kindness programs and share ideas worldwide. It was launched in 2000, involves many nations, and has a general assembly that meets every few years.[3] However, the type of movement I am talking about needs to be massive. It has to engage all members of our communities from young to old and call for our participation everywhere we turn.

It can be done. We have successfully implemented a vast movement on this scale in the past with the modern environmental movement of 1970, so we can do it again. In 1970, a US senator from Wisconsin, Gaylord Nelson, was inspired by the antiwar movement led by students across our nation. After an enormous oil spill in California, he knew that if he combined student energy with society's growing awareness of water and air pollution, it would give environmental protection attention on a national political stage. The modern environmental movement got the support of both Republicans and Democrats in the '70s and is still alive today.[4]

For fifty years, we have taught our kids about environmental concerns and raised their awareness about the need to protect and preserve our planet, thereby creating an environmentally conscious generation. My kids used to reprimand me if I got a grocery bag for a small item, used a plastic straw, or let the water run while brushing my teeth. I have already shared how Nick would sometimes pick up garbage lying around in public places, even while on vacation. I consider Kelli an environmentalist and often wonder if she will go into environmental law when she graduates from law school.

Kids celebrate Earth Day every April 22 in schools, town halls, park districts, scout meetings, and other venues by doing things like planting trees, conducting science experiments, and learning how to compost. They get involved in recycling programs and learn about global warming, as well as alternative sources of clean energy.

If we can teach our youth to become aware of our planet's needs and how to take action to care for our earth, then they can also learn to become aware of the needs of humanity and how to take action to care for themselves and one another. The lessons must come on a grand scale, as a movement—the humanity movement. It must be a full-out movement that is carried out consistently, comprehensively, and universally. If only some of our schools, families, and communities step up while others ignore the need to respond, then the movement will fizzle out. Our young people need to have these lessons reinforced everywhere they turn.

Just like Earth Day, the humanity movement can have its special day that we celebrate annually. We can call it Hearts for Humanity Day, Humans Day, Humans for Humanity Day, Humane Humans Day, or whatever else people decide to call it. We already have a World Suicide Prevention Day, an excellent day of awareness, but it involves a narrower focus, and preschoolers and early grade school children often have limited observance due to the age appropriateness of the topic. People of all ages, however, can participate in a Hearts for Humanity Day.

On that day, kids can get involved in organized service projects for others; create arts and crafts on humanitarian topics; conduct small, random acts of kindness; or attend age-appropriate talks about mental health from guest speakers. This will be more than raising awareness with a celebration for just one day: it will continue throughout the year—just as we don't stop recycling and conserving energy for the 364 days following Earth Day. Everywhere our children go, they are constantly reminded to not litter, to shut off lights, to reuse lunch bags, and to recycle. Recycling bins are placed in school lunchrooms and classrooms, as well as in malls, theaters, and churches. When kids go home, they see these bins in their garages, and the recycling trucks in front of their homes show them that their parents and towns also support the modern environmental movement. Kids hear talk about being "green" at school, on television, and from their community leaders; see solar panels installed on public buildings and private homes; watch windmills turning in fields as they ride along in their parents' energy-efficient cars; use water-saving toilets at home and in public restrooms; and collect pop tabs at home to bring to school for aluminum recycling.

We integrate the modern environmental movement into the daily lives of our children, and they are active and willing participants. They learn how important it is to participate, and they see the benefits of their actions. The humanity movement can be just as widespread and have the same impact and success with our children.

Just as we teach kids to conserve water and plant trees, let's help them understand what it feels like to be left out of a group activity, what goes through the mind of a child who sits alone at lunch each day, or how a kid who is always picked last during gym class really feels. We can teach them about the effects of bullying and, conversely, how acts of kindness can affect a child's life. At some point, possibly in sex education classes, we can teach kids that a person's sexual orientation and identity is a private matter, not a topic for ridicule. Let's also explain that it is not only inappropriate but cruel to try to "out" someone. People should not have to worry about sharing who they are with others.

We must teach kids that actions have consequences. That if you say mean and hateful things to someone, it can have a deadly impact. And for the love of God, we have to explain why it is *never* all right to tell someone, "Go kill yourself." When this happened to Nick, I thought it was just one aberrant, offensive comment said by a peer, but I have since learned that kids frequently say this to one another.

One of the fruits of the humanity movement must be to encourage adults to have open dialogues with kids about mental health. In age-appropriate ways, we need to define what mental health is and teach them what some of the signs of mental illness look like so they can better recognize if these develop in themselves or someone else. We need to teach them about having a healthy support system and the importance of reaching out to others when they feel depressed or need help in some other way. We must talk about loneliness and assure our kids they are never alone.

These are some of the concepts we can teach, but how do we bring the humanity movement forward and provide kids with these valuable lessons? Psychologists and teachers know, developmentally, when it is best to teach kids each of these topics. They are the experts who can work together to create a framework that will encompass all kids from the time they walk into preschool or kindergarten. We can teach these virtues through resources like books, games, videos, field trips, school assemblies, poster contests, class assignments, and extra-credit opportunities. Teachers and parent volunteers can observe and step in at lunch, gym class, and recess to help kids learn how to be kind and suggest ways to include others.

For very young kids, teachers can read stories and extrapolate them to real-life hypotheticals and scenarios involving topics such as bullying and being left out of activities. Many excellent teachers are already engaging young students this way by doing things like asking how the characters of a book might be feeling or how the student might help that character in real life. Recently I saw on the news how one kindergarten class in Fort Worth, Texas, assigns a new student each day to be the greeter who welcomes classmates with a "good morning" and a handshake or a hug when they show up for class. At only five years of age, these kids are already learning how it feels to be welcomed and included as part of something bigger than themselves, as well as how it feels to be on the receiving end of such goodwill. The kindergarten teacher who created this program said she believes starting each day this way teaches the kids compassion and respect for one another.[5] Let these teachers and schools who are already doing this type of work be an example for others.

All families, schools, youth sports programs, community park districts, scouting programs, faith organizations, and every other person or group that can influence children need to be part of the humanity movement and help teach these lessons starting from the earliest age possible, a time when kids are impressionable and easily motivated. If they grow up consistently hearing positive messages of caring and respect for others everywhere they turn, then the lessons learned will become a way of life. And if we all hold the humanity movement at least as necessary as the modern environmental movement of 1970, then it too shall be successful. Don't we owe that to ourselves? Don't we owe it to our children, especially when suicide is the second leading cause of death for ages ten to thirty-four? Think of that little nine-year-old boy in Colorado who took his life after being bullied by his classmates for coming out to them as gay . . . enough is enough.

The significant increase in suicides, mental illnesses, bullying, exclusion, and other acts of unkindness we see today is a multifaceted problem for sure, but if we bring the humanity movement forward to our youth, help kids be kinder to one another, and teach them about mental health, then we can save lives. And if we combine the humanity movement with lessening the pressure on them, as I described earlier in this chapter, then we will save even more lives.

Parents, do not rely on schools and youth programs alone to teach these lessons to your kids. You must be their partners and carry the humanity movement into your homes. You are not only at the forefront for teaching your kids these virtues, but keep in mind that you are also their primary role models. When you act, little eyes are watching. If you conduct yourselves selflessly, treat others with respect, and accept and appreciate people's differences, then your children will too.

Teach your kids how to love and care for themselves because if they cannot do that, they will have difficulties being kind, loving, and caring toward anyone else. Then, teach them those lessons of kindness, compassion, empathy, and inclusion in your own way. Just like the schools, you have to introduce these virtues at the youngest age possible. I tried to teach my kids those lessons in ways that would be fun for them.

When Nick and Kelli were very young, I loved taking them on long walks by our town's Riverwalk. As they sat side by side in their little wagon, I would ask them to close their eyes and tell me everything they heard and felt as I pulled them along the trail. They would describe things like the warm sun on their faces and the wind blowing in their ears. They told me they heard birds chirping, locusts buzzing, and water hitting against the shoreline of the DuPage River. Nick and Kelli were learning to use their senses to notice things outside themselves.

As they got a little older, around five and seven, I started bringing them to a nursing home filled with elderly residents with particular needs so they could begin developing empathy and compassion for others. The residents enjoyed their weekly visits, especially those who did not have grandkids. Kelli befriended a man with diabetes whose legs were amputated. At first, I thought the sight of him sitting in a wheelchair with no legs would frighten her, but surprisingly, even at such a young age she showed empathy and asked to visit him each week.

One day, as the kids listened to one of the residents share stories about his past, he told them how much he used to love White Castle hamburgers. He said it had been years since he'd had them. At the end of our visit, my kids looked at me with big eyes and asked if we could surprise him with some that afternoon. I remember it was sweltering hot that day and all I wanted to do was get home and into air conditioning, but how could I pass up the opportunity to teach my kids what it felt like to do a random act of kindness for someone? So, from the nursing home parking lot, we got into our minivan and drove to White Castle. It was very moving to see the joy on their little faces when they handed a bag of "sliders" to that resident. Nick and Kelli talked about it for days.

I cannot say enough about how taking my young kids for visits to the nursing home was instrumental in fostering their growth into kind, loving, and compassionate people. As a side note: the prohibition of bringing anything nicknamed "a slider" to an elderly person with a health condition probably should be a Law of the Universe, don't you think?

Another way I taught my young kids compassion and empathy involved writing prompts. When my kids were in early grade school, I often had them do small writing exercises during their summer breaks that required them to think a little outside the box and, more importantly, a little outside themselves. I would tear ads from magazines to use as prompts. For example, if the ad depicted two men in a boat with a ball sitting on the seat between them, I would ask my kids to imagine they were the ball and then write about how it felt sitting next to the two men. They never had to write much, just enough to have them think outside themselves and about feelings, all while using their imaginations and creativity. Of course, there were no wrong ways to respond to those prompts. The goofier I made them, the more my kids would laugh.

Whenever Nick and Kelli came home from school and told me about how some kid did something inappropriate or acted up at recess or in the classroom, I would ask them how that child must have felt to do something like that. I asked them their thoughts about how their peers reacted and responded the way they did. I even asked how the teacher felt about it all. Basically, I threw a lot of questions at them requiring them to consider people's feelings and the reasons and emotions behind actions. I wanted my kids to get used to thinking about those things regularly and heighten their sensitivity to the needs and feelings of others.

These are just a few examples of how I tried to teach Nick and Kelli to be kind, empathetic, and compassionate. You will find what works best with your kids, all while creating beautiful memories along the way. Any time invested in your children is well worth every moment.

If we want a kinder society, we must start with the youngest members and build from there. I am hopeful for our future. I think kids are tired of all the stress on them and have been greatly affected by losing so many of their peers to suicide. They are aware that a change is needed and know things cannot continue as they are now. They are onboard. Now it's up to us to help them with that change. It is time for the humanity movement to begin.

Chapter 19

Final Stories of Hope

"Do small things with great love."

—Mother Teresa

will leave you with two heartwarming, true stories that exemplify how each of us can make a difference in someone's life. We can help others in many ways without having to carry out some grand humanitarian effort like traveling the world on a mission trip. We just have to look outside ourselves and notice how others are acting or behaving. If we see signs of distress or get a gut feeling that something is a little off, then we need to reach out and take action. We tend not to want to step forward, though, because we wonder, "What if I'm wrong? What if I'm not reading the situation correctly?" The answer is to err on the side of caution and take action. If you are wrong, at least you showed that person you care. The real question we should all be asking ourselves is, "What if I'm right but do not act?"

STORY ONE: STAY HERE, MY FRIEND

About three years ago, I had just finished getting the Nick's Network of Hope website up and running and wanted to make people aware of the information and resources it contained. Everywhere I went, I handed out cards with the charity's name and website on them, even at our dog groomer's shop. About a month later when I returned for my dog's next grooming, the young woman behind the reception counter told me almost matter-of-factly, "Oh, I think your website saved my friend's life a few weeks ago. Would it bother you if I told you about it?" I answered, "Of course not."

She explained that one morning while she was sitting at the reception desk by the front counter, there was a lull in customers dropping off their pets, so she decided to go on Facebook to pass the time. On her News Feed, she noticed a posting made by her friend that morning saying he had given up and was going to take his life that day.

Her friend, in his twenties, was estranged from his family and lived in a very rough neighborhood in Chicago. He had been fighting depression for a while and had reached out to her one other time when he was contemplating suicide. She was able to run to his side and persuade him to change his mind, but this day, she was panicking because she could not leave work to be with him.

Her mind raced as she tried to figure out what she could do from work to stop him. Then suddenly she remembered the cards I handed out a few weeks earlier. They had been sitting in the bottom drawer of the reception desk. Although she never went online to check out the website listed on the cards (nicksnetworkofhope.org), she knew it had something to do with suicide prevention. In desperation, she took a picture of one and forwarded it to her friend instructing him to spend time browsing the website before he did anything.

She waited anxiously but did not hear from him until the end of her workday. He called to tell her that after going through the site, he decided to *stay*. Her friend never mentioned what he saw there that inspired him to change his mind. He just said he no longer wanted to give up and was going to continue fighting to live.

Thanks to that receptionist's quick thinking and action, that young man lived. She did not brush off his post as some Facebook drama or cry for attention, but rather took his words seriously. She acted quickly and reached out with helpful information and resources. Her actions showed him how much she cared and, more importantly, saved his life.

The ending gets even happier. I contacted this young man soon afterward, and we became friends. He is a kind, intelligent person with a beautiful spirit and a big heart. Presently, he is working six days a week at two jobs and says he is "very happy." He doesn't have "negative thoughts anymore" and makes sure he surrounds himself with positive people, like his new girlfriend, who he says is a big blessing in his life. He told me he greatly appreciates that people were there to motivate him to get healthy— and he did.

STORY TWO: ELEVATOR FRIENDS

The second story involves my daughter, Kelli. In the summer of 2018, she was working in Chicago in a high-rise that faced the Chicago River. A cluster of suicides happened over about a two-week period right around where she worked. More than once, the employees in her high-rise looked out their windows and saw the Chicago police dredge the river for a body. The morale of some workers was low those couple of weeks as they talked among themselves about the suicides.

One morning as the police were searching for a body to retrieve, Kelli texted me saying how difficult it was for everyone in her building to concentrate on work with everything going on around them. Kelli decided to go out for lunch that afternoon and take a long walk far away from the river to get a break from it all. Returning to her lobby, she got in the elevator with a gentleman she had never seen before. He was in his late thirties or early forties. As they rode in silence, Kelli noticed he looked upset. Knowing how disturbed people were over the sudden rash of suicides, she asked, "Are you all right?" He looked at her and burst into tears. "The stress is too much," he said, shaking his head. With that, the elevator doors opened, and he walked down the hallway to his office.

Kelli kept thinking of this man after she returned to her office on another floor. She was worried about him and decided to reach out to make sure he was going to be all right. Sitting at her desk, she wrote him a quick letter that began, "Kind Man From Floor . . ." Kelli then confided that she lost her brother to suicide five years ago, and that experience now makes her more aware of the feelings of others. She added how she has since learned that life struggles and blessings tend to even out, so she knew things would get better for him. The entire rest of the letter was filled with hope and encouragement. Kelli told him he now had a new friend, and she was available if he ever needed to talk. She signed the letter giving him her floor number and some final words of support, "Best wishes, warm waves of kindness & prayers." She put her note and a bag of Skittles in an envelope and went back to his floor to figure out where he worked. As she handed the envelope to him, he said just two words, "Thank you." It was Friday afternoon and a pleasant way for both of them to end a very long week.

The following Tuesday morning, when Kelli arrived at work, a beautiful bouquet of summer flowers was sitting at her desk with a card from—you guessed it—the man in the elevator. In the card, he thanked Kelli for her kindness and expressed how it touched his heart in such a way it took a few days to process. He added, "You have no idea how powerful that moment meant for me and to me." He said a million things were going through his head, and the stress was wearing him out. He thanked Kelli for "noticing and having the heart to embrace the moment." He continued, "I know God is real, and he continues to prove himself by putting us in the right place at the right time." Then he signed the card, "Your Elevator Friend," with his signature and floor number.

What a perfect example of how a small act of kindness can really make a difference in someone's life. (Another Law of the Universe.) It can make someone smile, feel cared for, find hope, and appreciate self-worth. It can even save a life. Kelli was just as uplifted from his kindness as he was from hers. Their interaction reflects the goodness in humankind.

We hear many negative stories in the news about gender and race discrimination. Well, here is an example of two people who could not have looked more different from the outside if they tried—Kelli is a petite white woman, and her new friend is a tall black man. Nevertheless, their kindness and compassion for one another transcended any physical difference. None of the other stuff mattered that day—and never should. What counts is what is inside *all* of us. We are all humans. We have the same wants and needs. We want to feel part of something bigger than ourselves and need to be loved. We want to live a life free of pain and stress. And when we recognize in others a need for care and restoration to balance, it is up to us to step forward and help in any way we can.

We must all focus on *Saving Ourselves from Suicide* because we *can* save ourselves and one another. If you are having thoughts of ending your life, save yourself by reaching out to people around you. Yell for help to get the piano off your chest. If you are doing well but notice someone else is being bullied, looks distraught, or in some other way seems to need help, then step out of your comfort zone and take action. Minding your own business is not being kind or compassionate. We must all try our best to save each other from suicide. That is the business of us *all*.

If someone you knew, and perhaps loved, has taken his or her life, do not let that tragedy multiply by also taking you down. You can save yourself from *that* suicide by doing things like relying on your faith, joining a support group, forgiving others, and eventually training your brain to think more positively—which includes forgiving yourself for signs you may have missed or things you think you should have said or done.

It is up to all of us to be life preservers for one another. We must learn to love ourselves and one another, regardless of our differences, and teach our youth virtues like kindness, empathy, compassion, and inclusion. We are all in this life together, so let's make it a better tomorrow.

> *The greatness of humanity is not being*
> *human, but in being humane.*
>
> —Mahatma Gandhi

Acknowledgments

Special thanks to:

- ❀ Tom and Kelli Pacha, for your love and support. Thank you for your willingness to sacrifice our privacy by agreeing to share our story to help others. I love you both very much.

- ❀ Ann Mahalko, for being my wonderful mother and companion in prayer whenever Nick had difficulties and my rock after he passed. I miss you, Mom.

- ❀ My extended family and all our wonderful friends who loved and supported Tom, Kelli, and me throughout our grief. You are a blessing in our lives.

- ❀ George Pappas, for your wisdom and integrity.

- ❀ Debbie Zaccarine, Charlotte Bunce, Rudy Radasevich, Fr. Paul Hottinger, Rev. Dr. Scott Mitchell, Sue Greco Costello, and Debbie Perry-McMullen, for graciously volunteering your time and talents to read my manuscript and offer advice.

Reading Group Discussion Questions

I f you are in a reading group or plan to form one, I have created a list of discussion questions that relate to the content of *Saving Ourselves from Suicide*. We can all do our part to reduce the stigma associated with mental health issues and suicide by talking about these topics with others. Sharing your thoughts and reactions to my son's story and the subjects addressed throughout this book is a good starting point for conversation.

To download the list of questions, please go to the Nick's Network of Hope website (nicksnetworkofhope.org).

Thanks for reading and sharing.

Linda

Additional Resources

In Crisis

I f you are in crisis, please reach out to the National Suicide Prevention Lifeline at 800-273-8255. If talking on the phone makes you uncomfortable, you can reach a crisis counselor at the Crisis Text Line by texting TALK to 741741 (United Kingdom: text 85258, Canada: text 686868).

Please remember that you do not have to be suicidal to use these services. You may just want an empathetic ear or to ask what you can do to help someone else you think is suicidal.

You can also find additional resources on the resources page at Nick's Network of Hope (nicksnetworkofhope.org).

Suicide Loss Survivors
(Friends and Family after a Completed Act of Suicide)

If you are a suicide loss survivor, please go the resources page at Nick's Network of Hope for additional information.

Please Tell Others and Consider Writing a Review

Thank you for reading this book. If you like it and think someone else would benefit from it, please share the title with them. Another way this book can get into more hands and help more people is by you leaving a review on Goodreads and on the retailer site where you purchased the book. Even a line or two would make all the difference and would be appreciated.

All Net Proceeds from Sales Will Benefit Suicide Prevention

All net proceeds from the sale of *Saving Ourselves from Suicide*, authored by Linda Pacha and published by AutumnBloom Press, will be distributed by both entities to Nick's Network of Hope. Nick's Network of Hope is a 501(c)(3) nonprofit whose mission is to provide resources, education, and support about life challenges with an emphasis on mental health awareness, suicide prevention, and grief and loss. AutumnBloom Press is wholly owned and operated by Nick's Network of Hope and is formed for the purpose of producing educational resources in support of Nick's Network of Hope's mission. Linda Pacha is the founder/ president of Nick's Network of Hope.

Nick's Network of Hope
We bring hope, awareness and understanding.
nicksnetworkofhope.org

Notes

Chapter 1: Losing a Child: A Metaphorical Look

1. Aaron Rupar, "Stone Arch Bridge Suicides: Teenage Couple Jump to Their Deaths Days after They Go Missing," *City Pages*, May 31, 2013, http://www.citypages.com/news/stone-arch-bridge-suicides-teenage-couple-jump-to-their-deaths-days-after-they-go-missing-updates-6548984.

2. Andy Greder, "Roseville Teacher Died in Jump from Minneapolis Bridge," *Pioneer Press*, MediaNews Group, May 28, 2013, https://www.twincities.com/2013/05/28/roseville-teacher-died-in-jump-from-minneapolis-bridge/.

Chapter 2: Mental Health Issues and Suicide Can Happen in Any Family

1. Natasha Tracy, "Difference between Mental Illness and Mental Disorder," HealthyPlace.com, May 20, 2018, https://www.healthyplace.com/other-info/mental-illness-overview difference-between-mental-illness-and-mental-disorder.

2. American Psychiatric Association, *Diagnostic and Statistical Manual of Mental Disorders*, 5th ed. (Arlington, VA, 2013), 20; Dalena van Heugten-van der Kloet and Ton van Heugten, "The Classification of Psychiatric Disorders According

to DSM-5 Deserves an Internationally Standardized Psychological Test Battery on Symptom Level," *Frontiers in Psychology*, August 4, 2015, https://doi.org/10.3389/fpsyg.2015.01108.

Chapter 3: Nick's Story

1. Lisa Jo Rudy, "Does Asperger Syndrome Still Exist?," Dotdash, updated November 22, 2018, https://www.verywellhealth.com/does-asperger-syndrome-still-exist-259944.

2. Jamie Freed, "Living with an Asperger Profile for Adults," Asperger/Autism Network (AANE), accessed January 5, 2019, https://www.aane.org/living-asperger-syndrome-adults/.

3. Julie Marks, "Asperger's Syndrome: What Are the Signs and Symptoms of the Disorder?," Everyday Health Group, updated March 22, 2018, https://www.everydayhealth.com/aspergers/what-are-signs-symptoms-disorder/.

4. Carol Bainbridge, "The Meaning of the IQ Test Score," Dotdash, updated September 21, 2019, https://www.verywellfamily.com/meaning-of-iq-test-scores-1449360.

Chapter 6: The Memorial Service

1. "Suicide," in *Catechism of the Catholic Church: Revised in Accordance with the Official Latin Text Promulgated by Pope John Paul II*, 2nd ed. (Washington, DC: United States Conference of the Catholic Bishops, 1997), Flipbooks Edition, 550, #2282, http://ccc.usccb.org/flipbooks/catechism/files/assets/basic-html/page-I.html#; Paul McKibben, "Suicide: What Does the Church Teach? Resources to Help Those in Need," *Catholic Digest*, June 8, 2018, http://www.catholicdigest.com/wellness/body-soul/suicide-what-does-the-church-teach-resources-to-help-those-in-need/.

2. "Can Catholics Who Commit Suicide Be Given a Catholic Church Burial?," Catholic Charities Diocese of Cleveland, October 22, 2014, http://cqrcengage.com/ccdocle/app/document/4808104?04 (reprint of article by Right Rev. Joseph Osei-Bonsu originally posted on Vatican radio website; Bonsu article removed from website).

Chapter 8: Bullying and Social Difficulties

1. Eli Meixler, "Denver Mom Says Her Nine-Year-Old Boy Killed Himself after Homophobic Bullying at School," *Time*, August 28, 2018, http://time.com/5379876/denver-9-year-old-suicide-bullying/.

Chapter 9: Stigma and Complexities of Mental Health

1. Suzanne Baker, "Judge Dismisses Lawsuit Alleging Police, School District Contributed to Naperville North Student's Suicide," *Naperville Sun-Chicago Tribune*, January 22, 2019, https://www.chicagotribune.com/suburbs/naperville-sun/news/ct-nvs-suicide-lawsuit-dismissed-naperville-st-0123-story.html.

2. Stacy St. Clair, "School Disciplinary Incident Ends with a Naperville Teen's Suicide: 'They Scared Him to Death,'" *Chicago Tribune*, May 23, 2017, https://www.chicagotribune.com/news/local/breaking/ct-naperville-north-suicide-20170522-story.html.

3. Suzanne Baker, "Naperville District 203 Agrees to Pay $125,000 to Walgren Family to Settle Wrongful Death Suit," *Naperville Sun-Chicago Tribune*, September 10, 2019, https://www.chicagotribune.com/suburbs/naperville-sun/ct-nvs-203-walgren-settlement-st-0911-20190910-wceadjsu6 bfipgpz62ue4u3f7m-story.html.

4. Baker, "Judge Dismisses Lawsuit."

Chapter 10: Social Landmines

1. Cynthia Waderlow, "Children's Autonomy during Grief," *Loving Outreach to Survivors of Suicide (LOSS) Newsletter*, Catholic Charities, October 1, 2016, http://catholiccharities.net/tabid/472/vw/1/itemid/959/children%E2%80%99s-autonomy-during-grief.aspx; Waderlow, "Grief and Family Development: Grieving over Time," *Loving Outreach to Survivors of Suicide (LOSS) Newsletter*, Catholic Charities, April 1, 2014, http://catholiccharities.net/tabid/472/vw/1/itemid/423/grieving-over-time.aspx; and for grade school age children, see also Waderlow, "School Age Children and Their Grief Processes," *Loving Outreach to Survivors of Suicide (LOSS) Newsletter*, Catholic Charities, May 1, 2015, http://catholiccharities.net/tabid/472/vw/1/itemid/848/school-age-children-and-their-grief-processes.aspx.

Chapter 13: A Matter of Faith

1. Betty J. Eadie, *Embraced by the Light* (Placerville, CA: Gold Leaf Press, 1992), 104.

2. Mary Fairchild, "What God's Grace Means to Christians: Grace Is the Undeserved Love and Favor of God," Dotdash, https://www.thoughtco.com/meaning-of-gods-grace-for-christians-700723.

3. "Grace: What It Is and What It Does," Catholic Answers, November 19, 2018, https://www.catholic.com/tract/grace-what-it-is-and-what-it-does.

4. Good News Translation.

5. "Grace," Catholic Answers.

Chapter 14: Choices, Changes, and Self-Growth

1. Associated Press, "Parents of Boy Killed by Alligator at Disney Launch Transplant Program," *Fox News*, September 27, 2017, https://www.foxnews.com/health/parents-of-boy-killed-by-alligator-at-disney-launch-transplant-program.

2. "Welcome to WISQARS," Centers for Disease Control and Prevention, National Center for Injury Prevention and Control, Web-Based Injury Statistics Query and Reporting System (WISQARS) [online], accessed September 2019, www.cdc.gov/injury/wisqars.

Chapter 16: Risk Factors and Warning Signs

1. T. Dazzi, R. Gribble, S. Wessely, and N. T. Fear, "Does Asking about Suicide and Related Behaviours Induce Suicidal Ideation? What Is the Evidence?," abstract, *Psychological Medicine* 44, no. 16 (December 2014): 3361–63, doi: 10.1017/S0033291714001299.

Chapter 17: Things to Know to Help Yourself and Others

1. Nancy Schimelpfening, "How to Create a Suicide Safety Plan," Dotdash, updated January 3, 2020, https://www.verywellmind.com/suicide-safety-plan-1067524.

2. The website for the National Suicide Prevention Lifeline, SAMHSA, https://suicidepreventionlifeline.org.

3. Dazzi, Gribble, Wessely, and Fear, "Does Asking About Suicide and Related Behaviours Induce Suicidal Ideation?"

Chapter 18: A Better and Safer Tomorrow

1. Paul D. Polychronis, Peter F. Lake, "Overreacting to College Student Suicide?," Inside Higher Ed, May 16, 2018, https://www.insidehighered.com/views/2018/05/16/colleges-should-not-expect-suicide-be-100-percent-preventable-opinion; Ronnie Walker, "Is Suicide 100% Preventable? Probably Not," *Alliance of Hope* (blog), August 2014 and April 2012, accessed September 2014, https://allianceofhope.org (blog post deleted by March 26, 2019).

2. "Welcome to WISQARS."

3. The website for the World Kindness Movement; the "About Us" page, http://www.theworldkindnessmovement.org/about-us/.

4. "The History of Earth Day," Earth Day Network, accessed September 10, 2018, https://www.earthday.org/ history.

5. Genevieve Shaw Brown via GMA, "Kindergarten Handshake Ritual Is Kids 'Favorite Part of the Day,'" *ABC News*, May 30, 2018, https://abcnews.go.com/GMA/Family/teachers-meet-greet-routine-making-manners-matter-texas/story?id=55513728.

About the Author

Linda Pacha has firsthand knowledge of the devastation caused by a loved one's suicide and the excruciating pain from losing a child. In 2013, her teenage son, Nick, died by suicide while away at college. Using the insights gained from his painful life, his tragic death, and her personal grief journey, Linda founded Nick's Network of Hope, a 501(c)(3) nonprofit that provides resources, education, and support about life challenges with an emphasis on mental health awareness, suicide prevention, and grief and loss.

Linda is an attorney. Prior to receiving her law degree, she obtained a BS in psychology and completed one year of postgraduate studies in clinical psychology. She is a public speaker and spends her time helping others as founder/president of Nick's Network of Hope (nicksnetworkofhope.org), fulfilling the nonprofit's mission. Linda has donated her time being a pastoral care minister for the homebound and a religious education teacher for school-aged children, holding these positions for more than ten and fifteen years, respectively. She lives with her family in Naperville, Illinois.

Please follow Nick's Network of Hope on Facebook.